CORINTHIAN CORRESPONDENCE

CORINTHIAN CORRESPONDENCE

Ministering in the Best
and Worst of Times

Helen Doohan, PhD

WIPF & STOCK · Eugene, Oregon

Wipf and Stock Publishers
199 W 8th Ave, Suite 3
Eugene, OR 97401

The Corinthian Correspondence
Ministering in the Best and Worst of Times
By Doohan, Helen
Copyright©1996 by Doohan, Helen
ISBN 13: 978-1-5326-0648-9
Publication date 8/18/2016
Previously published by Resource Publications, Inc., 1996

Contents

Acknowledgments ix

Introduction 1
Paul's Background
Paul's Call
The Letters of Paul
The Focus of This Book

1. Paul and the Corinthian Church 11
   History and Background of Corinth
   Paul's Relationship with the Corinthian Church
   Religious Influences on Paul and the Corinthian Community
   Paul's Coworkers and Colleagues in the Early Church

2. The Corinthian Correspondence 37
   The Letters of Paul to the Corinthian Church
   Paul the Writer

3. Paul's Gospel 63
   Paul's Proclamation of the Gospel
   Understanding of God in the Corinthian Correspondence

4. The Corinthian Church's Life and Value Systems 83
   Households of Faith and the Local Church
   The Understanding of Church in the Letters to the Corinthians
   Corinthian Issues and Their Impact on Ecclesial Life

5. Liturgical Interests in the Corinthian Community 111
   Celebrations in the Corinthian Church

6. The Ministry of Disciples in the Corinthian Letters . . . 133
   Disciples, Apostles, and Missionaries in 1 and 2 Corinthians
   Living Out the Call in the Corinthian Church
   Essential Aspects of Mission and Ministry in Corinth
      and Beyond

7. Celebrating in New Times and Places 159
   Cycle A
   Cycle B
   Cycle C

Afterword: Ministering in the Best and Worst of Times . . . 189

Resources 193

Index of Scripture References 199

Index of Authors Cited 207

Index of Subjects 209

Acknowledgments

Special thanks to Julianne Dickelman and Rocky Morrow for their research assistance, to Gonzaga University for a sabbatical opportunity to complete the manuscript, and to my husband, Leonard, and daughter, Eve-Anne, for their unconditional love, encouragement, and support.

Introduction

> It was the best of times, it was the worst of times, it was the age of wisdom, it was the age of foolishness, it was the epoch of belief, it was the epoch of incredulity, it was the season of Light, it was the season of Darkness, it was the spring of hope, it was the winter of despair, we had everything before us, we had nothing before us, we were all going direct to Heaven, we were all going direct the other way—in short, the period was so far like the present period, that some of its noisiest authorities insisted on its being received, for good or for evil, in the superlative degree of comparison alone.
> Charles Dickens, *A Tale of Two Cities*

The apostle Paul could have written the above words about the church in Corinth and his relationship to it. Instead he says: "Grace to you and peace from God our Father and the Lord Jesus Christ. I give thanks to my God always for you because of the grace of God that has been given you in Christ Jesus" (1 Cor 1:3-4). While Paul uses a typical greeting in the opening of his letter to this Christian community, his relationship with them is anything but ordinary and his feelings less than grateful and calm. As

Introduction

we will discover in our reading of the Corinthian letters, it is the best and the worst of times, a season of hope and a season of despair for both Paul and the Corinthian church. Will these letters also echo our own experience of church and ministry? In this correspondence we glimpse the interaction between the early church and the Gentile world and identify the church's struggle to live the Gospel preached to them by Paul. We also witness the development of the apostle's long and frustrating relationship with a community that is inquisitive, enthusiastic, energetic, and knowledgeable. Passivity seems unheard of in Corinth!

In many ways the Corinthians are very much like Paul himself, and we will identify some of their similarities as we examine the biblical text. Paul and the Corinthians also seem very much like ourselves in their struggle to make sense of their commitment in a culturally and religiously diverse environment. Their experience of church also resonates with ours, as we both attempt to reinterpret the Gospel message for new times and places, and in the process please some and alienate others. What brings Paul to his missionary activities in Corinth? How do these letters compare with others written by the apostle or sent later in his name? What do these Corinthian letters contribute to our understanding of the early church? What are the connections between then and now? What part do these texts and their message play in our liturgical celebrations today?

Paul's Background

Two sources provide the major material available to us for the background of Paul, his own letters and Luke's Acts of Apostles. While these sources must be used differently since the former come from the apostle himself in the decade of the 50s and the latter are attributed to the historian and theologian Luke, writing in the late 80s or early 90s, they concur on many points regarding Paul's life and ministry. In some instances, Acts expands our knowledge of the details of Paul's life and his journeys on behalf of the Gospel.

Paul describes himself as "circumcised on the eighth day, a member of the people of Israel, of the tribe of Benjamin, a

Hebrew born of Hebrews" (Phil 3:5), "advanced in Judaism beyond many among my people of the same age" and "far more zealous for the traditions of my ancestors" (Gal 1:14). Luke identifies his Jewish background as a native of Tarsus (Acts 9:11; 21:39; 22:3), Roman citizenship (16:37-38; 22:25-29; 23:27), and education under Gamaliel in Jerusalem (22:3). Both speak of Paul's Pharisaic background (Phil 3:5; Acts 23:6; 26:5) and his persecution of the church (1 Cor 15:9; Gal 1:13.23; Phil 3:6; Acts 8:1.3; 9:1-2.4-5.13-14; 22:7-8). Paul's conversion, with its revelation of Jesus as risen Lord, is pivotal for his understanding of Christ and Christians, and sets his missionary direction toward the Gentiles. Paul's subsequent founding of churches on his major missionary journeys (Acts 13-21.27-28) are well documented. The apostle's contacts with Jerusalem and its leaders (Gal 2:1-10) and his confrontation with Peter in Antioch (Gal 2:11-21) offer a picture of interaction in the early church. Personal difficulties and various imprisonments (2 Cor 6:5; 11:23-29), as well as Paul's continued work at a trade (1 Cor 9:3-19; Acts 18:3) give this part-time missionary an aura of extraordinary accomplishment and unbounded energy. We can imagine the apostle continuing as a leather worker while preaching the Gospel and enduring the difficulties of travel as well as the struggles of ministry in a time of transition. However, Paul himself puts his life and work in perspective when he speaks of having "this treasure in clay jars, so that it may be made clear that this extraordinary power belongs to God and does not come from us" (2 Cor 4:7).

The Corinthian letters give us some indication of the strengths of the apostle but offer a different perspective from Luke. "For they say, 'His letters are weighty and strong, but his bodily presence is weak, and his speech contemptible'" (2 Cor 10:10). Luke presents Paul as a great speaker, yet fails to acknowledge his letter writing and major theological insights. However, Acts and letters, when taken together, offer a composite picture of one of the key figures in the early church.

Additional information comes to us from an apocryphal writing, the Acts of Paul and Thecla, in which we find this description of Paul:

Introduction

> And he saw Paul coming, a man little of stature, thin haired upon the head, crooked in the legs, of good state of body, with eyebrows joining, and nose somewhat hooked, full of grace: for sometimes he appeared like a man, and sometimes he had the face of an angel (as quoted in Kee 168).

This description may shatter our image of the apostle, but no less so than the portrayal Paul allows to come through in his letters, particularly Galatians, Philippians, and 2 Corinthians. The most personal portrayal of Paul emerges in these writings as he confronts and challenges a wayward community in Galatia, displays a loving and affirming approach to the Christians in Philippi while in prison, or moves to extremes of boasting and pleading in a continuing situation of misunderstanding in Corinth. Some scholars would comment on the embarrassing traits of his personality (Bornkamm 239), but still acknowledge that person and ministry go hand in hand (168). The human qualities of Paul, as they emerge in the Corinthian correspondence, allow us to see many aspects of his personality and encourage us to work with limitations and greatness as he did. However, the most significant aspect of Paul's life was his experience of Jesus as risen Lord and the transformational revelation it contained.

Paul's Call

The conversion of Paul is the central event for understanding his mission and theology. The events are familiar both from Paul's letters and Luke's three accounts from a single tradition. In both sources the writers interpret this religious experience in prophetic terms, with Paul relying heavily on Jeremiah's account of his call. The following table identifies major references to Paul's call and some parallels in the Jewish Scriptures.

TABLE 1: PAUL'S CALL/CONVERSION EXPERIENCE

PAUL'S LETTERS	ACTS OF APOSTLES	PARALLELS IN THE JEWISH SCRIPTURES
Gal 1:11-16	Acts 9:3-20	Jer 1:5-10
1 Cor 15:8-9	Acts 22:6-17	Isa 49:1-6
2 Cor 4:6	Acts 26:12-19	Isa 52:6-16
1 Cor 9:1	Acts 13:47	Ezek 2:1
Phil 1:12-14; 2:16		
Rom 15:20-21		

Several significant factors should be kept in mind when reflecting on Paul's call. As a Pharisee and a dedicated Jew, Paul was exceptional in his commitment to the God of Israel, being involved in missionary activity and interpreting the Law in a more expansive way than other religious groups within Judaism of his day. The fact that he was a diaspora Jew—that is, living outside Palestine—gave him a perspective on life that included the Gentiles and a firsthand appreciation of Hellenistic thought patterns. The conversion, or call as it is more properly identified, occurs because of the initiative of God and contains elements of a refined understanding of the beliefs and mission of Paul. In this religious experience Paul encounters Jesus as risen Lord and understands the intimate connection between Christ and Christians. "He asked, 'Who are you, Lord?' The reply came, 'I am Jesus, whom you are persecuting'" (Acts 9:5). His understanding of Christ and of God's action in and through Christ on behalf of humankind changes, and Paul now directs his sense of mission to the proclamation of the Gospel as apostle to the Gentiles.

Subsequently, Paul reflects on this transformational experience, and his letters indicate a theological development based on his initial insights in this revelation. The Corinthian letters also indicate the continuing conversation between Paul's theology and the community's questions and needs. Likewise, these letters reveal how Paul translates and interprets a Jewish Gospel for a Hellenistic environment, and the integration of past beliefs with his present religious convictions. The conversion, or Paul's second call, attests to the apostle's ability to change and to refocus on essential issues in his life of faith. In this respect, Paul can be a model for us as we grow in maturity in our Christian lives.

The Letters of Paul

While we will examine the Corinthian correspondence in detail in chapter 2, a perspective on Paul's other letters will enable us to see these texts within the larger framework of New Testament writings. Only seven letters undoubtedly come from the apostle himself. These authentic letters are 1 Thessalonians, Galatians, 1 and 2 Corinthians, Romans, Philippians, and Philemon. Many commentators question the authorship of letters such as 2 Thessalonians, Colossians, and Ephesians because of language, style, theology, and setting. The pastoral letters, 1 and 2 Timothy and Titus, unquestionably come from a period later than Paul because of their vision of church, content, and style. The following table indicates the authentic letters and the degree of questioning of authorship of the other letters written in Paul's name.

TABLE 2: LETTERS OF PAUL AND AUTHORSHIP

AUTHENTIC LETTERS OF PAUL	AUTHORSHIP QUESTIONED IN DESCENDING ORDER
1 Thessalonians	2 Thessalonians
Galatians	Colossians
1 & 2 Corinthians	Ephesians
Romans	Pastorals (1 & 2 Timothy; Titus)
Philippians	
Philemon	

Ideas of authorship differ from biblical times to the present day with the early writers focusing more on the validity and authentic interpretation of the message than on the actual writer. The ending of Romans indicates the use of a secretary, Tertius (16:22), and the opening of some letters, such as 1 and 2 Corinthians suggests co-authorship by Sosthenes and Timothy respectively. Later biblical authors write "in the tradition of" Paul, and utilize his name in the opening of their letters, such as in Ephesians, 1 and 2 Timothy, and Titus. Identifying authenticity, or authorship, and approximate dating of letters enables us to interpret their context and pursue reasons for their particular development of earlier ideas or apparent contradictions. Analyzing the integrity of the letters, or asking the question whether text is in the same form as it was originally written, opens other possibilities for understanding the message. Insertions into letters and composites of several letters into one occur in the New Testament. Corinthians will offer us ample opportunity to explore the construction of the text so that we can better understand its meaning then and now. This aspect will be particularly important for the SCRIPTURE IN WORSHIP & EDUCATION series as readers attempt to reinterpret the biblical message in the context of worship and religious education for the communities they serve.

Introduction

The Focus of This Book

The Corinthian correspondence and the community it reflects are exciting and exasperating, interesting and complex. We come in touch with an urban environment, with a Greek milieu, and with Paul's ministry to this vital church over a period of several years. The letters offer us a window of opportunity to view Paul's personal and pastoral presence in his growing relationship with this church. Struggling with his own history, the history of the community, and the newness of the Gospel he preaches, Paul identifies an approach that balances tradition and innovation, theological foundations and principles for action. With Paul's letters we move away from the rather ideal portrayal of the early church associated with Acts of Apostles to a realistic and unpolished portrayal of community development in this period. The passion, persuasion, and purpose of the apostle permeate these letters, and no one is unaware that the Lord Jesus is the center of his Gospel message and of his life. In addition, these letters reveal the earliest theological reflection available to us, and unfold the lifestyle and interests of disciples of the Lord.

In order to explore issues in the Corinthian correspondence that will illuminate our understanding of Scripture and focus the liturgical preparations of readers of this series, I offer the following approach in this book.

The early chapters will focus on the background of Corinth and Paul's relationship to the community (chapter 1), the development of the letters and an approach to their style, interests and themes (chapter 2), and the origin and content of Paul's Gospel (chapter 3). Then we will examine the place of the households of faith, the understanding of church, the values and issues that emerge in these letters (chapter 4). Liturgical interests (chapter 5), discipleship, Christian life, and ministry (chapter 6) will round off our perspective on Paul and the Corinthian community. Finally, a commentary on specific liturgical readings (chapter 7) will hopefully enhance the usefulness of this book for religious educators, liturgical ministers, and inquiring believers.

Introduction

I began this introduction with a quotation from *A Tale of Two Cities*. Dickens poignantly referred to London and Paris during the French Revolution, but his description could span centuries and well apply to Corinth in biblical times and to your community today. In fact, while this book focuses on the Corinthian correspondence, my own appreciation of these letters goes beyond the experience of Paul and the early church to the insight they offer to Christians in the contemporary church. Indeed the best of times and the worst of times are still with us as we struggle for freedom, equality, truth, and justice. The contrasts within Dickens' description—wisdom/foolishness, belief/incredulity, light/darkness, hope/despair, heaven/hell—describe his reality, the Corinthian situation, and our own experience of church as well. Echoes of Paul's Corinth and his intensely personal and frustrating relationship with the community reverberate into our century, and can offer insight and encouragement to those of us who take the time to read, study, reflect, and reinterpret the biblical text. These pages will allow us to begin the journey of discovery as we immerse ourselves in Paul's time, so that comparisons can be made between then and now.

Chapter One

Paul and the Corinthian Church

Great figures often take their place in history because of what they do and what others remember about them. Individuals like Jesus and Paul did not create their times but responded to their situations in extraordinary ways, leaving their impact on the generations that followed them. Jesus so influenced Paul that the apostle became the missionary of the early church whom we all remember and the writer who still challenges us by his words and commitment. Paul's missionary journeys took him to exciting parts of the world filled with intellectual inquiry, religious cults, philosophical schools, and a marvelously diverse social milieu. The Corinthian correspondence allows us to glimpse some of Paul's work in this environment and to identify the earliest remembrances of Jesus by Christians. However, understanding Paul and the Corinthian correspondence is no easy task for their world is so different than ours. Placing these letters and Paul's relationship to the Corinthian community within their historical context enables us to appreciate, more fully, their power and complexity.

Strands of the history of Corinth in the centuries before Paul can be reconstructed from ancient writings and archeological findings, and this evidence will set the stage for viewing Corinth in New Testament times. A perspective on Corinthian life, culture, and social structures enhances our appreciation of the diversity of issues and interests that engage this church and its apostolic founder. Paul interacts with this community through visits, letters, and reports from key figures in the church, offering us a glimpse of travel patterns and social relationships in the biblical period. In addition, converts in Corinth bring their previous religious backgrounds to their Christian faith, understanding of the Gospel, and new lifestyles. Their broad interests emerge as Paul, his coworkers, and the community come to life in the exciting pages of 1 and 2 Corinthians. We will examine these aspects of the Corinthian world and Paul's relationship to the Corinthian church in this chapter.

History and Background of Corinth

Ancient Corinth

The beginnings of the mythical history of Corinth and its people can be traced back thousands of years before the common era (BCE). Actual settlements existed in the area some four thousand years BCE, but the period of interest to us begins with the establishment of colonies in the eighth century BCE. Corinth became a major power in Greece by the fifth century, although its position fluctuated with its naval supremacy (Papahatzis 17-18). Its life and culture developed in Hellenistic times until its complete destruction by the Romans in 146 BCE. Approximately one hundred years later, the city was rebuilt by Julius Caesar and reinhabited by soldiers, freedmen, merchants, business people, and settlers from various parts of the empire, becoming the thriving cosmopolitan center that Paul visited.

As capital of the province of Achaia (27 BCE), Corinth developed as a commercial center with its share of trade, banking, and government administration. The city was also known for art, crafts, and Corinthian bronze, a metal more precious than gold, with some of its unearthed treasures dating from the sixth century BCE. In his letters, Paul uses these images known to his audience, such as the earthenware jar (2 Cor 4:7) and the sounding brass and noisy gong (1 Cor 13:1).

Ancient writers offer testimony to the prestige of Corinth and its reputation. In a fascinating book, *St. Paul's Corinth*, Jerome Murphy-O'Connor gathers the testimony of historians, philosophers, and other writers of the intertestamental period to offer us a glimpse of the glory and enigma of this city. For example, Cicero, writing from his firsthand experience, called Corinth "the light of all Greece," even though he saw the city in its dark period, probably 79-77 BCE. He could identify the potential of its natural advantages and is the only eyewitness from the period to indicate the ruins were not completely deserted (46-48). However, the sacking of Corinth by the Romans was a tragedy of major proportions. Paintings and other works of art were treated with disregard by the army, according to writings of Strabo, who used an eyewitness account of Polybius (203-120 BCE) in a now lost manuscript (64). But Strabo (ca 63 BCE-15 CE), a scholar with interests in historical geography, also spoke of "the favourable position" of Corinth and of terra-cotta reliefs, bronze vessels, and earthenware taken from the ruins and graves (66). Corinth seemed to be an ideal place for economic development in the century before Jesus and Paul, accounting, in part, for its refounding and reconstruction. Pliny the Elder (23-79 CE) described the quest for Corinthian bronze as a "wonderful mania" (86), indicating the city's continued artistic reputation into the time of Paul.

However, beyond the arts, the archaeological remains of the ancient city allow us to reconstruct this urban center. Corinth itself was spacious, with grassy and open areas within its parameters. Remains of city walls, colonnades, baths, theaters, temples, roads, homes, and shops allow the modern visitor to imagine everyday life in this stimulating environment. Speakers or visitors, like Paul, would address audiences at the *bema*, or speakers platform, in the center of the marketplace, and the small shops would provide work areas for the apostle as he continued in his trade. This thriving city suffered a massive earthquake in 77 CE, necessitating extensive reconstruction, and so the site visited today contains ruins from several periods in Corinth's history, reflecting Greek and Roman influences. Just as the history of this city affected its inhabitants in Paul's time, so too the history of our cities affects our communities as we proclaim and interpret the Gospel message.

Geographic Location

A major factor in the growth of Corinth is its geographic location, as our maps of the area indicate. Located fifty-five miles west of Athens, Corinth is just beyond a narrow stretch of land, or isthmus, four miles wide and ten miles long that connects the mainland of Greece and the leaf-shaped Peloponnese. The Gulf of Corinth lies to the west of the isthmus, and the Saronic Gulf, opening to the Aegean Sea, is on the eastern end. As early as the sixth century BCE, plans were discussed for a canal spanning these two bodies of water that would provide a sea route from east to west. Efforts moved forward under Nero in 66 CE with several thousand workers digging at Isthmia for more than three months. However, construction was not resumed until 1881, and the canal officially opened in 1893 (Papahatzis 29). In biblical times, a road allowed transport of travelers and their ships between the two gulfs. This arduous journey for those involved provided a shorter and less dangerous route to Italy.

The port cities of Lechaeum, Isthmia, and Cenchreae were important to Corinth, and we know that Paul travelled by ship from Cenchreae, a city associated with Phoebe, the deaconess (Rom 16:1), and probably visited there frequently. Lechaeum was the nearest port to Corinth and was connected with it by long walls made of limestone and brick in the fifth century BCE. According to Pausanias, the city contained a temple and a bronze statue of Poseidon, god of the sea, and, according to Plutarch, a sanctuary to Aphrodite, the goddess of love, fertility, and beauty (Papahatzis 45).

Isthmia was famous for the panhellenic Isthmian games, celebrated every two years and possibly attended by Paul during his visits to the area in 49 and 51. These games were second in importance to the Olympic games; others were celebrated at Delphi and Nemea. According to ancient sources, women participated in the events, possibly explaining the liberated women in the Corinthian church (Murphy-O'Connor, *St. Paul's Corinth*, 16). The prize or crown in ancient times was a wreath of celery, later replaced by a wreath of pine. Paul uses the imagery of the games when he says to the Corinthians: "Do you not know that in a race the runners all compete, but only one receives the prize? Run in such a way that you may win it. Athletes exercise self-control in all things; they do it to receive a perishable wreath, but we an imperishable one" (1 Cor 9:24-25). Isthmia, which was the site for the games, contained a sanctuary to Poseidon, originally dating from the seventh century BCE. It was rebuilt for the fourth time with the restored city of Corinth in 44 BCE (Papahatzis 30).

The city of Corinth itself was impressive. The Acrocorinth, an imposing citadel, and its centerpiece, the temple of Aphrodite, rose more than 1,886 feet above the lower city, providing a backdrop and a defense. Corinth itself had a temple of Apollo, god of sunlight, prophecy, music, and poetry, as well as temples of other deities. The agora or

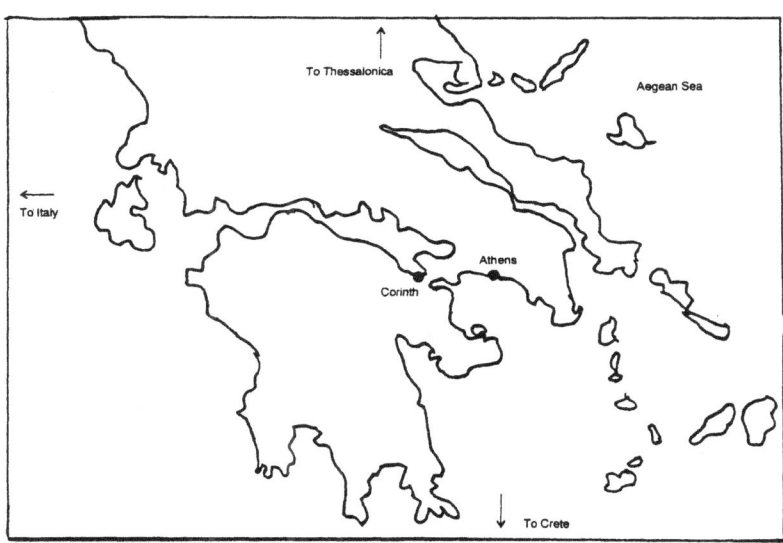

Map of the Corinth and Surrounding Areas

marketplace with its fascinating shops and structures, a theater for about 14,000 persons, gymnasium, utilities, and other public buildings insured a vital center for its civic, social, and economic life. A layout of the urban area gives a sense of the relationship of places and allows us to imagine Paul in this bustling city.

Corinthians, viewed as living without constraint, had a well-earned reputation in sexual matters. "To act like a Corinthian" meant to practice fornication and "a Corinthian girl" described a prostitute. While these descriptions probably suited some of Corinth's history, sacred prostitution was not a Greek practice, and the Corinth of New Testament times was probably no worse than other port cities of the period (Murphy-O'Connor, *Corinth*, 56). However, Paul does refer to sexual immorality in his letters to the community, indicating issues that needed attention. Corinth also had a history of factions, and divisions would plague the apostle in his dealings with the community (Welborn 110-111).

The history, geography, culture, economics, religion, and political importance of Corinth certainly had an impact on the New Testament community of Paul's letters. However, in the apostle's time, many of the citizens would have only a sense of their recent past as they lived in the newly rebuilt city that had an air of excitement and fulfillment. The caution of C.S. Lewis could apply: "The unhistorical are, usually without knowing it, enslaved to a fairly recent past" (quoted in O'Meara 97). This could well apply to ourselves and the communities we serve, living two thousand years after the time of Jesus and Paul.

Corinth in the Time of Paul

When Paul arrived in Corinth, he would have entered a thriving center of crafts and commerce, a center of worship of Aphrodite, an active and enterprising community. In his encounters, Paul would come in profound contact with the Greek mentality, its intense curiosity and independence of mind. Quick judgments, appreciation of knowledge and wisdom, and sophistication in worldly matters would characterize the tenor of the city. In this metropolis of as many as 600,000 inhabitants in Roman times, Paul had the possibility of influencing people from many different areas, and he could also work at his trade with business from travelers, visitors for the Isthmian games, merchants, and ship's crews. The bustle of the city would be attractive to this urban missionary and his enthusiasm would be matched by theirs.

The city contained open areas near its walls and some very beautiful and desirable places to live, such as Craneum. The remains of a Roman villa at Anaploga can be dated to the time of Paul, and a comparable household would be the

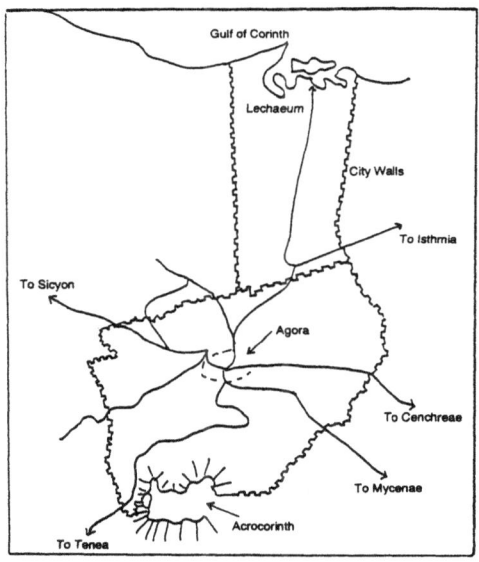

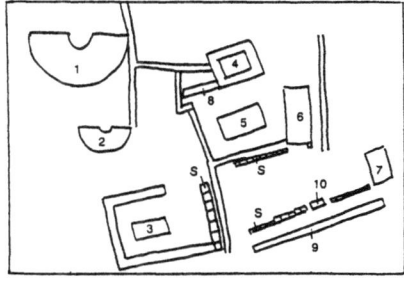

THE AGORA AT CORINTH AROUND THE YEAR 50:
1. Theatre
2. Odeion
3. Temple
4. North Market
5. Temple of Apollo
6. Basilica
7. Basilica
8. North Stoa
9. South Stoa
10. Bema
S. Shops

The City of Corinth

gathering place for the celebration of the Lord's Supper (1 Cor 11). Although the space in such a villa was reasonably large, forty or fifty people would constitute overcrowding and they would overflow into other rooms, accounting for some of the problems Paul addressed (Murphy-O'Connor, "Corinth Paul Saw" 157). As you moved away from the wealthy areas, you would notice crowded conditions in most dwellings and a lack of privacy (Meeks 28-29). Paul would use this city and its homes as a base for his ministry, since Athens was no longer the center of Greek life and culture. The socially diverse and stratified society, with its wealthy and poor, powerful and powerless, reflected the times and would challenge Paul in his preaching of the Gospel.

Paul's Relationship with the Corinthian Church

Paul and the Corinthian Christians

Paul visits Corinth during his second missionary journey, travelling to the city after leaving Athens, and proclaiming the Gospel to a group that quickly embraces the faith. As founder of the church, Paul has special ties to the community which he maintains through visits and letters. "For though you might have ten thousand guardians in Christ, you do not have many fathers. Indeed, in Christ Jesus I became your father through the gospel" (1 Cor 4:15). However, this relationship does nor guarantee mutual understanding. The letters adequately document Paul's strained relationship, veiled hostility on both sides, and, at times, open rebellion. Paul is overly sensitive to misunderstanding and opposition, as 2 Corinthians indicates, and he often boasts about his credentials and ministry. He writes of "distress and anguish of heart," asks them if "we are beside ourselves...in our right mind," and pleads with them to "open your hearts to us," for he feels "a divine jealousy" for them. He finally says "I hope you will find out that we have not failed" (2 Cor 2:4; 5:13; 7:2 11:2; 13:6). On the other hand,

Murphy-O'Connor speaks for many: "Conceited, stubborn, over-sensitive, argumentative, infantile, pushy. All these adjectives have their place in a description of the Corinthian Christians for whom Paul was responsible" (*I Corinthians* ix). The apostle continually works at maintaining good relationships with the community and, in this, becomes a model for us in our ministry.

These interesting aspects of the underlying relationships between Paul and the church must be complemented with the content of the letters, which leave us with a balanced theology and a first glance at the interpretation of Jesus' message some twenty years after his death.

Social Stratification in the Community

The most interesting aspect of Corinth in Paul's time was the internal social stratification of the community (Theissen 98). Paul recalls this fact in an early section of 1 Corinthians: "Consider your own call, brothers and sisters: not many of you were wise by human standards, not many were powerful, not many were of noble birth" (1 Cor 1:26). While this passage has often been interpreted to demonstrate the appeal of the Gospel to the ordinary and poor in the early stages of Christianity, the community was a cross-section of the city which consisted of one third full free citizens, one third freedmen, and one third slaves (1 Cor 7:21-23). People of different social levels were brought together because of their faith in the Gospel. As Meeks notes: "The churches, too, were mixtures of social statuses. The kinds of relationships that members previously had to one another, and still had in other settings—between master and slave, rich and poor, freedman and patron, male and female, and the like—stood in tension with the *communitas* celebrated in the rituals of baptism and the Lord's Supper" (191).

Paul would be immersed in the richness and diversity of social life as he walked the streets of Corinth. The message he preached would attract people from every social rank, and so Paul would emphasize solidarity and fundamental equality before God in his approach to the community. This realistic solution to a potential problem allows for pluralism within the context and ideal of Christian love. The implications of such teaching for relationships within the household structure were astounding. In fact, these faith communities would become alternative environments to the prevailing societal norms of status and gender roles within hierarchical structures.

We can wonder if Paul understood the full implications of his message for women, slaves, and poor as he pondered the Corinthian situation. However, he does take this courageous step, and he emphasizes change in relationships within the community of faith to reflect that "all are one in Christ" (Gal 3:28; 1 Cor 12:13). External structures do not seem to be as much of a concern to the apostle, rather, he focuses on community life. This insight offers us a possible approach in our ministry.

During Paul's time in the city, he would notice the wealth of the Corinthian citizens and their upward economic and social mobility. Some of the conflicts that Paul encountered in Corinth had economic and social dimensions for "the most active and most important church members probably belong to a small group of Corinthian Christians with high social status" (Holmberg 104). He challenged this community to renounce titles and honors that belonged to them, a radical departure from first-century attitudes to religious organization (Banks 136). Interestingly enough, the status of women was positively affected by their acceptance of the Gospel and insertion into an egalitarian faith community. On the other hand, Paul's own status decreased with his conversion for he lost authority and prestige in the eyes of the world in his embrace of hardship and powerlessness.

The reality of social stratification affected the church, and Paul deals with the tensions, struggles and implications of this environment in his preaching and his writing. While we may have different views of class and status than the Pauline Christians, these aspects of life affect our social relations and our daily choices. They impact our liturgical celebrations and our community life causing distancing or separation among church members, a factor considered by Paul and by ministers today. Likewise, social context affects the biblical text itself in its language, style, issues, and perspective. Understanding its influence will allow us to uncover the original meaning of the text and reinterpret it for communities that share radically different values and world view.

Paul's Visits and Chronology

Two sources provide information on Paul's visits to Corinth, with the journeys in Acts of Apostles establishing a larger framework for the specific references in 1 and 2 Corinthians. According to Acts 18:1-3, Paul left Athens during his second missionary journey and went to Corinth. There he met and worked with Aquila and Prisca (Priscilla), who were expelled from Rome under an edict of Claudius. According to Luke, Paul preached in the synagogue, stayed with Titius Justus, who lived next door to the synagogue, and converted and baptized Crispus, a synagogue official, and all his household (Acts 18:4-8; 1 Cor 1:14). He remained a year and a half in Corinth until he was brought before Gallio, the proconsul of Achaia (Acts 18:11-17). This reference to Gallio is the most verifiable chronological source since an inscription found at Delphi in conjunction with other references narrows the date of his proconsulship between 50-52 CE, probably as early as 50-51 (Murphy-O'Connor, *Corinth* 141-152; "Corinth Paul Saw" 148). References to Felix, Procurator of Judea between 52-59 (Acts 23:24-26), and Festus, Procurator of Judea between 60 and 62 (Acts 24:27; 25:1), account for other reasonably verifiable dates.

After his sojourn in Corinth, Paul set sail for Syria and then reached Ephesus, accompanied by Aquila and Prisca (Acts 18:18-19). His travels continued while Apollos went to Corinth (Acts 18:24-19:1; 1 Cor 3:6), and after a period of time, Paul decided to return to Macedonia and Achaia. He then planned to continue on to Rome (Acts 19:21). The apostle finally returned to Corinth during his third missionary journey, which took him again to Greece (Acts 20:2).

In his own letters, the apostle refers to visits and letters that enable us, along with Acts, to reconstruct a tentative chronology. Paul speaks of his founding visit to Corinth and his preaching of the Gospel (1 Cor 2:1-3; 3:2). He also identifies the relationship between himself and Apollos. "I planted, Apollos watered, but God gave the growth" (1 Cor

3:6). When unable to visit, Paul sends Timothy to Corinth (1 Cor 4:17; 16:10) with the intention of revisiting the community soon and spending some time with them (1 Cor 4:19; 11:34; 16:2-7). Having written a previous letter to the Corinthians (1 Cor 5:9), Paul then addresses issues that he hears from Chloe's people and questions he receives from their letter to him (1 Cor 1:11; 7:1). Paul, in our 2 Corinthians, refers to his second visit, "So I made up my mind not to make you another painful visit" (2 Cor 2:1), and to another letter he wrote to the church "out of much distress and anguish of heart" (2 Cor 2:4; possibly referring to 2 Cor 10-13), that caused the community pain (2 Cor 2:3-4.9; 7:8.12). After these difficult encounters, Titus arrives with news and consolation (2 Cor 7:6.14-15), and the apostle indicates that he will send Titus, his partner and coworker, to the Corinthians again with another brother known to them (2 Cor 8:16-19).

In our text of 2 Corinthians, Paul describes his approach to the community in his letter writing and visits: "I myself, Paul, appeal to you by the meekness and gentleness of Christ—I who am humble when face to face with you, but bold toward you when I am away!" (2 Cor 10:1). He does not want to frighten them with his letters (2 Cor 10:9), but reminds them again of his founding visit (2 Cor 10:14). Paul then recounts the perils of his ministry in the rest of this letter, and speaks of his readiness to visit a third time (2 Cor 12:14; 13:1.10). Other places are mentioned in the correspondence, such as Macedonia (1 Cor 16:5; 2 Cor 1:16), Troas (2 Cor 12:12), and Ephesus (1 Cor 16:8).

While we can easily gather references to letters and visits, determining the chronological framework is difficult. Paul probably wrote at least four letters to the Corinthian church and visited three times for reasonably long periods of three to eighteen months. Discussion continues among scholars about the order of the letters; for example, was 2 Corinthians 10-13 written before chapters 1-9? We will examine this issue later. The dating of the edict of Claudius is also open to question. Conclusions are difficult since Paul himself mentions only one event linked to general history, that Aretas was king of the Nabateans during his early problems in Damascus (2 Cor 11:32) (Murphy-O'Connor, *Corinth* 129-140).

The following table identifies the various components that contribute to the picture of Paul's relationship to the Corinthian church and offers a usable chronology for our purposes. While differences regarding Pauline chronology prevail, a framework for his ministry enables us to see the development in his relationship with this church. Other details will be added as we look at the development of the letters and their content.

TABLE 3: CHRONOLOGY AND EVENTS

EVENTS	LETTERS	REFERENCE	DATE
Conversion		Acts 9, 22, 26	34-37
Edict of Claudius		Acts 18:2	41 or 49
First Missionary Journey		Acts 13:1 -14:28	46-49
Second Missionary Journey		Acts 15:30 -18:22	?50-53
First (founding) visit to Corinth (18 months); conversion of household of Stephanus; baptism of Crispus and Gauis; work with Aquila and Prisca		Acts 18:1-3.11; 1 Cor 2:1-5; 3:5-6: 1:14.16	50-51
Gallio, Proconsul of Achaia		Acts 18:12-17	51 (50-52)
Felix, Procurator of Judea		Acts 23:23; 24:27	52-59?

Third Missionary Journey	Letters written to Corinthians	Acts 18:23-21:17	53-58
	Lost Letter (A) 1 Corinthians (B)	1 Cor 5:9 1 Cor 16:18	51-54 54
Second visit to Corinth; painful visit		2 Cor 13:2 Acts 20:2 2 Cor 2:1-4	54
	Lost Tearful Letter (C)	1 Cor 7:8-11	54-55
	Letter of Reconciliation (?) 2 Cor 1-9 (D)		55
	Harsh/Angry Letter (?) 2 Cor 10-13 (E)	2 Cor 2:3-4.9; 7:8-12	56
Third Visit to Corinth			56
Departure to Jerusalem		Acts 21:17	57-58
Portius Festus, Procurator of Judea		Acts 25:1	?60-62
Journey to Rome		Acts 27:1-28:16	59-60?
Death of Paul			?62-64

Paul's founding of this church implies a profound relationship with them and a recognition of his authority for building up their faith (2 Cor 13:10). As an apostle, Paul attempts to persuade the Corinthians to modify their behavior, beliefs, and attitudes in accord with the Gospel he preaches. We read his challenges in the letters and we witness his struggles to grow with this community over a long period of time. This correspondence offers hope and insight to Christians today who minister within the same community for extended periods of time.

Religious Influences on Paul and the Corinthian Community

Variety of Religious Influences

With the vitality Corinth displayed as a cosmopolitan city, we can well imagine the spirited level of religious inquiry, influences, and practices. Various philosophical currents of thought permeated the atmosphere; Hellenistic ideas and thought patterns prevailed; religious rituals and cults were part of life. A major city like Corinth would have a sizable Jewish population, as would all the Pauline communities, even though Paul's letters do not explicitly mention contact between the Christians and the Jewish synagogue (Meeks 168). Because of these factors, the Corinthians would be familiar with Jewish Scriptures and teaching, as well as Greco-Roman ideals and ideas. Paul uses imagery from these various traditions in his preaching and writing, and in this approach, translates a Palestinian-based Gospel for a Gentile audience.

The apostle himself brings an interesting background to his missionary work. Born in Tarsus, a city known for its Stoic school, Paul appreciates the Stoic sense of purpose in the universe, personal detachment, inner equality, and freedom. These ideals underlie many of Paul's comments in his letters (Phil 4:12; Gal 3:28; 1 Cor 12:13; 2 Cor 4:8-9; 12:9; 13:9). He also understands the mystical and relational elements of the mystery religions with their rites and rituals that have counterparts in Christian celebrations (1 Cor 11:26; Rom 6:2-4). Language and ideas associated with the seeds of Gnosticism permeate Paul's thought as he attempts to clarify his theological understanding (1 Cor 6:16-17; 15:40-44). Likewise, the apostle is keenly aware of the attribution of divinity to great figures, the growing appreciation of monotheism, sensitivity to dying and rising from observation of the cycles of nature, and sense of personal communion with the divine in the Greek and Roman world of his day. Paul's awareness of these religious developments tempers his use of language and sharpens his categories of thought as he preaches the Gospel in this Gentile environment (1 Cor 1:20-22; 10:20; 2 Cor 4:4). He readily identifies with the spiritual quest of the Corinthians from his own religious commitment and experience of the risen Lord.

However, Paul also brings his strong Jewish heritage to the Corinthian church. "Are they Hebrews? So am I. Are they Israelites? So am I. Are they descendants of Abraham? So am I" (2 Cor 11:22). His missionary activity, belief in resurrection and afterlife, and interpretation of Scripture come from his Pharisaic background. Paul appreciates and understands the Gentile world from his own experience as a diaspora Jew. Jews living outside Palestine accounted for close to six million people in the first century. In addition, the apocalyptic tendencies of later Judaism, with its focus on the end times, are part of Paul's preaching and theological development.

Paul assumes familiarity with the approaches of Greek thought and Jewish ways in the Corinthian community. Their intensity and enthusiasm allowed them to appreciate the diversity of approaches that various religious traditions offer. Syncretism, a blending of various religious elements into the practice of one's own faith, usually has negative connotations in this period. However, in the Corinthian church, this tendency contributes to the pluralism and diversity that emerge in the letters. This richness provides the opportunity for a new interpretation of the good news in a very exciting culture. We discover similar situations in many of our communities today.

The background of the Corinthians prepares them to embrace a new teaching of wisdom and knowledge and to generate enthusiasm about the gifts of the Spirit, but they have difficulties with resurrection of the body and preaching of the cross. Rather than hope in future life, these Christians prefer to enjoy spiritual ecstasy in the present, a real concern for Paul in his teaching on the end times. Radically different eschatological views are at stake. These religious differences, along with social stratification, contribute to the conflict Paul encounters in the church.

The letters indicate how the community makes transitions from one stage in its understanding to another, a key to its religious integration and, perhaps, its survival. Acknowledging and accepting different perspectives of belief is a perennial challenge, and liturgy frequently reflects successes and failures for it incorporates theology and practice in its rituals. Therefore, sensitivity to religious influences and cultural diversity will enhance our ability to facilitate the growth of a faith community. This was as true for Paul as it is for ourselves.

Community Interests in Corinth

The background and situation of the Corinthians give rise to the major interests that emerge in the pages of Paul's letters to the church. These interests reflect the religious heritage of the church, daily life in this thriving urban area, and the desire to bring these elements together in response to the Gospel message preached by Paul. These Christians are "a community struggling with developmental problems which we would expect of a young community whose beliefs and way of life differed sharply from the bustling urban environment in which it had been planted" (LaVerdiere 69).

The Corinthians are enamored by prestige, eloquence, brilliance, wisdom, mystical experience, and religious enlightenment. Their expectations are shaped by their experiences in the marketplaces, political and philosophical discussions, exciting ideas from visitors around the empire, and exposure to outstanding speakers. The tone of the opening chapters of 1 Corinthians and Paul's discussion of wisdom reflect these influences on the community. In addition, wisdom, knowledge, power, and wealth continue to be important to these Christians even after their conversion, and the apostle will challenge their perspective (1 Cor 1:17-26). The community is also concerned about Spirit possession and spiritual gifts, giving importance to speaking in tongues (1 Cor 14:4-19) and prophesying (1 Cor 11:4-5). However, Paul presents a different view of spiritual gifts and their place in the community (1 Cor 12:28-31).

Leadership in the community, and its association with prestige, eloquence, and power, is another Corinthian interest. "So let no one boast about human leaders. For all things are yours, whether Paul or Apollos or Cephas or the world or life or death or the present or the future—all belong to you, and you belong to Christ, and Christ belongs to God" (1 Cor 3:21-23). These Christians value their connections with various preachers (1 Cor 1:12), and Paul attempts to understand them. However, he speaks of apostleship in very different terms and boasts of the extent of his own commitment to ministry on behalf of the churches in stark contrast to leaders the Corinthians emulate (2 Cor 10-11). This view of leadership and authority has implications for community gatherings (1 Cor 11:18-19) and indicates a reliance on prevailing social structures rather than transformation in Christ (2 Cor 5:17).

Some of the Corinthian interests underlie the questions they address to Paul in the letters, such as those concerning marriage and celibacy, food to idols, and spiritual gifts (1 Cor 7:1.25; 8:1; 12:1). In addition, Paul has concerns regarding immorality, ethical behavior, divisions in the community, and the need for reconciliation (1 Cor 5:1.11; 11:18; 2 Cor 5:20). He speaks of order in the Christian assembly and the role of women in the churches (1 Cor 11:2-16; 14:27-36). The apostle also reflects on theological issues such as the community as the body of Christ (1 Cor 12:12), the resurrection of Christ and believers (1 Cor 15:12-15), and the meaning of Christ's death for Christian life and ministry (1 Cor 1:23-24). These comments, reflections, and challenges of Paul mirror the Corinthian situation and interests. Life in Corinth emerges in the letters as Paul clarifies issues, provides a context for interpretation, and offers principles for discernment to the community.

We can see that this church has many interests and poses exciting questions to its leaders. Their willingness to explore new areas of thought challenges the apostle to reexamine his theology and practice. In fact, the situation of the church determines Paul's exercise of leadership and his theological reflection (H. Doohan, *Leadership*, chapter 3). Knowing our communities, as Paul did, enhances our ability to respond appropriately and to celebrate effectively.

Paul's Coworkers and Colleagues in the Early Church

Partners in the Spread of the Gospel

Paul conveys great interest in the individuals who comprise the church in Corinth, and collaborates with coworkers and colleagues in the spread of the Gospel and community development. The names and descriptions of these individuals in the New Testament writings allow us to enter into the world of Jesus' disciples. These followers in the Pauline communities describe themselves and their mission: "For we are God's servants, working together; you are God's field, God's building" (1 Cor 3:9). We discover an interdependence among the coworkers in the proclamation of the Gospel, but Paul remains a focal point even though he extends his mission through others (Banks 162-163). These early disciples possess a vivid realization that God acts in and through them, and they rely on God's power for their effectiveness (1 Cor 12:4-5; 2 Cor 12:6; 13:3-4). The complex network of relationships that results in the early church is unparalleled in religious groups of the time and contributes to its rapid development and unity. We continue to find value in such networks in church life and ministry today, often spending time on enhancing their effectiveness.

The Scriptures indicate many names of these partners in mission and community leaders. Some of these figures are local community leaders, others converts of Paul, still others Christians from various churches who travel on their own, in pairs, or with the apostle. Ministries vary, from community organization and liturgical celebration, to preaching, teaching, and prophecy, according to the gifts and abilities of each person. The authentic letters of Paul name as many as forty coworkers, Acts identifies eight more, and the Pastorals an additional ten. Of these, 1 and 2 Corinthians mentions 17 and, these include 9 members of the upper class who travel extensively (Theissen 92). As impressive as their work is, Paul puts the efforts of all in perspective and indicates their equality and community support. "I planted,

Apollos watered, but God gave the growth. So neither the one who plants nor the one who waters is anything, but only God who gives the growth. The one who plants and the one who waters have a common purpose [are equal (RSV)], and each will receive wages according to the labor of each" (1 Cor 3:8).

Coworkers in Corinth

The pages of 1 and 2 Corinthians identify many outstanding individuals and their responsibilities in the community. The opening statement indicates the senders of the letter: "Paul, called to be an apostle of Christ Jesus by the will of God, and our brother Sosthenes" (1 Cor 1:1). Paul baptized a few community leaders, namely, Crispus, Gaius, and the household of Stephanus (1 Cor 1:14.16; 16:15), all members of the upper strata of society, who though a minority, exerted great influence in the community. Crispus was a synagogue ruler, as was Sosthenes (Acts 18:17-18). Gaius had considerable wealth, and his home could accommodate the whole church in Corinth (Rom 16:23). Paul praises Stephanus, his first convert in Achaia and patron of the church, and the apostle urges the church "to put yourselves at the service of such people, and of everyone who works and toils with them" (1 Cor 16:15-16). Stephanus is probably the person who brings the Corinthians' letter to Paul, along with other messengers, Fortunatus and Achaicus (Meeks 57-59.119). Verbal reports reach Paul through Chloe's people and, it is of interest in this period, that a delegation traveled under the name of a woman who was head of a household (1 Cor 1:11).

Another important leader in the Corinthian church is Apollos, an Alexandrian Jew, eloquent and "well-versed in the scriptures" (Acts 18:24) who came from Ephesus to preach the Gospel after Paul left Corinth. He is mentioned numerous times by Paul (1 Cor 1:12; 3:4.6.22; 4:6; 16:12) and in Acts (18:24-19:1), but no other record of his activity survives. The Corinthians appreciated Apollos' rhetorical ability, and while competitiveness existed between his followers and Paul's, the apostle acknowledges Apollos' work in the community. In fact, Paul puts the gifts of all leaders in perspective when he reflects on their call by God. "And

God has appointed in the church first apostles, second prophets, third teachers; then deeds of power, then gifts of healing, forms of assistance, forms of leadership, various kinds of tongues" (1 Cor 12:28).

Paul stays with three different households in Corinth, that of Gaius (Rom 16:23), Titius Justus (Acts 18:7), and Prisca/Priscilla and Aquila (1 Cor 16:19; Rom 16:3). We know a reasonable amount about his relationship with Prisca and Aquila a Jewish couple from Rome (Acts 18:1-2). If order of names indicates priority in relationship and esteem by the user, then Prisca is certainly esteemed by Paul who mentions her first, in contrast to Luke who varies his order (Acts 18:2.18.26). This couple are tentmakers, with whom Paul travels and works, and missionaries in their own right, who challenge Apollos in his understanding of the Gospel (Acts 18:25-26). Although described as coworkers, they have relative independence, as does Apollos, in the exercise of their ministry. Prisca and Aquila travel extensively, evangelizing Ephesus before Paul's arrival there, and supporting a church in their house (Acts 18:19.26).

Timothy and Titus are two important figures who work with Paul in Corinth and who are known to us from other New Testament writings. Timothy, son of Greek father and Jewish Christian mother (Acts 16:1-3) is undoubtedly the co-worker closest to the heart of Paul, and seems to have been his assistant for fifteen years (Holmberg 59). Paul remarks to the Corinthians "... I sent you Timothy, who is my beloved and faithful child in the Lord, to remind you of my ways in Christ Jesus, as I teach them everywhere in every church" (1 Cor 4:17). Although he was unsuccessful in this church, he has the trust and confidence of Paul and models his pastoral practice on that of the apostle. This may account for his difficulty, but Paul also understands the temperament of the Corinthians for he says: "If Timothy comes, see that he has nothing to fear among you, for he is doing the work of the Lord just as I am; therefore let no one despise him" (1 Cor 16:10-11). He and Silvanus are associates of Paul in the founding of this church; he co-authors 2 Corinthians (2 Cor 1:1.19) and 1 and 2 Thessalonians.

Titus is also a partner and coworker of Paul who ministers with Timothy on behalf of the apostle (2 Cor 8:22-23).

However, Paul makes an interesting comment about Titus when he says that he is going to Corinth "of his own accord" (2 Cor 8:17), suggesting the kind of commitment he has to the community and the level of his relationship to Paul. The Corinthians seem to respect Titus and his work (2 Cor 7:15-16). He is also the bearer of Paul's harsh and difficult letter to the church (2 Cor 2:12-13; 7:5-16), and arranges the collection (2 Cor 8:16-23). Titus accompanies Paul on his journey to Jerusalem (Gal 2:1-3), but Acts does not mention him. The Pastoral letters, written long after the time of Paul, are addressed to Timothy and Titus.

Mentioned with Timothy and Titus is Silvanus, the Silas of Acts, who accompanies Paul on his second missionary journey and works with him in Corinth (2 Cor 1:19; Acts 15:22). He is a leading member of the Jerusalem church, whose travels and imprisonment Luke relates (Acts 15:22-35). The letters to the Thessalonians also mention this figure in the early church (1 Thess 1:1; 2 Thess 1:1).

From the ending of the letter to the Romans, we learn that Tertius, a scribe, writes the text in Corinth (Rom 16:22), and Erastus is the city treasurer of Corinth (Rom 16:23; Acts 19:22; 2 Tim 4:20). Romans 16 offers the names of a host of coworkers in the churches. Paul speaks of Phoebe, for whom he uses the title *prostatis*, meaning "helper" or "patroness," who ministers in the church of Cenchreae, preaches, and teaches (Rom 16:1-2). Many other women labor and toil with Paul, including Junia, an apostle (Rom 16:7.12.15). Women exercise leadership in the early church, and Paul's inclusion of them in his missionary endeavors elevates their status in the community. The unnamed Corinthian women prophets and Paul's comments on the role of women in the church will be discussed later, but we cannot doubt the equality of women in the early mission of the church (Fiorenza 169; Gillman 63).

As we read through 1 and 2 Corinthians, we will notice how Paul, the coworkers, and the community interact. The names of these Christians remind us of individuals in the early church who are very much like ourselves in interests, vocation, and ministry. They contribute to the church in many ways—in a variety of ministries, by opening their homes to Paul and the community, with financial contributions, moral support, and, most importantly, with their generous commitment of time and their willingness to travel for the sake of the Gospel. These inspiring women and men are the predecessors of Christians today who take on similar responsibilities in their churches. The coworkers represent different levels of involvement, and they can encourage us in our work in the ecclesial communities of today.

As we reflect on Corinth, its history, Paul's relationship with the community, the religious influences and interests of the church, and some of the coworkers of the apostle, we cannot help but be impressed by the diversity and energy of this church. With this understanding of Paul and the Corinthians, we can examine the development of the letters and explore their meaning. A sense of history and knowledge of relationships continues to be critical for our churches today and we would do well to keep our own situations in mind as we reflect on Paul and Corinth.

For Personal and Group Reflection

1. The history and background of Corinth affected the Christian community, Paul, and his ministry in the church. What is the history of your city or town? How does it affect your community and ministry?

2. Corinth was a strategically situated, thriving city that became a vital center in the ancient world. Paul used this place as a center for his ministry. How does geographic location facilitate or hinder ministry in your church?

3. As founder of the Christian community in Corinth, Paul had a long and difficult relationship with the church. How would you describe the relationship between

religious leaders and community in your church?

4. The Corinthian church consisted of Christians of various economic means. How would you describe your community?

5. Paul utilized visits, letters, and coworkers to maintain and develop his relationship with the church. What are the ongoing and effective means of communication in your community?

6. Just as the Corinthian church experienced a variety of religious influences, so do Christian communities today. What are the religious influences in your area that affect the way you minister?

7. How would your describe the interests and needs of your community?

8. Paul had a cohort of workers to develop his mission in the early church. Who are the core of people in your community who are specifically engaged in ministry? How are they utilized by the religious leadership in the parish?

9. The impressive commitment of the early Christians challenges us to think about our own dedication to the Gospel. How do we express our commitment in terms of ministry? How are we partners in the spread of the Gospel?

10. Time and place provide the context for ministry. As we reflect on our times, our world, and our church, what do we see as

the primary challenges we face in our
Christian service of others?

Chapter 2

The Corinthian Correspondence

Paul's letters to the church in Corinth represent a significant portion of his *authentic* letters in the New Testament. Since they unquestionably come from the apostle himself, we can identify them as substitutes for his apostolic presence and part of his official acts as founder of the community. Within their chapters nestle theology, exhortations, greetings, travel plans, and personal insights into the life and ministry of Paul. Issues of importance to the Corinthian church also emerge as Paul creatively uses the typical Greco-Roman form of the letter to address the ever-changing situation in the community. It is important for us to keep in mind that the letters and contents are *occasional*; that is, they are specific to the Corinthian situation and to Paul's world. While they may contain theology, ethical principles, and pastoral insights for our church today, these can only be understood if we uncover and understand the original context, with its issues, concerns, and development. The correspondence, more accurately called *letters* than *epistles* since the sender, recipients, and situation are mutually known, provides an exciting view of a church in the first century. We can witness its growth, struggles, and pain as well as that of Paul, who first brought the Gospel message to this lively community.

Within 1 and 2 Corinthians in the New Testament canon, we can identify several visits and letters and discover their relationship to the factions and opposition Paul encounters in the Corinthian church. Although the *integrity*, or original form and order, of the letters is open to scholarly debate, 1 and 2 Corinthians are conversations that represent an ongoing dialogue between apostle and community. The purpose of each letter differs, but familiarity with the style of writing, terminology, and themes gives us the tools to understand the fuller meaning of the biblical text. This present chapter's outline of the material in 1 and 2 Corinthians will serve as a reference for the various sections of this book and as a guide for the context of readings used in our liturgical celebrations.

This correspondence reflects the details of growth of the Corinthian church and Paul's relationship to that community. It allows us to see subtle and concrete developments, positive and negative ways of handling situations, and, in so doing, offers hope to those of us who minister in questioning and energetic communities. Identifying with a church in crisis and a minister in a critical period of his apostolic work allows us to visualize alternatives to our own situation as church. As we travel with Paul and witness his attempts to maintain a relationship that seems overly susceptible to misunderstanding, we can appreciate moments of reconciliation and celebration in this faith community. Their journey as Christians then may speak to us now as we liturgically offer our prayers to God.

The Letters of Paul to the Corinthian Church

References to Letters and Visits in 1 and 2 Corinthians

The previous chapter presented a chronological chart on Paul and Corinth, combining the information gleaned from the two letters and Acts. In this section we will use data from 1 and 2 Corinthians to identify the actual development, number, and order of the letters the apostle wrote to this church.

Paul begins his letter to the Corinthians with the typical form of introduction of his day: "Paul, called to be an apostle of Christ Jesus by the will of God, and our brother Sosthenes, to the church of God that is in Corinth, to those who are sanctified in Christ Jesus, called to be saints, together with all those who in every place call on the name of our Lord Jesus Christ, both their Lord and ours: Grace to you and peace from God our Father and the Lord Jesus Christ" (1 Cor 1:1-3). Although called 1 Corinthians in our bibles, we soon discover this is the second letter of the apostle to Corinth, and that his previous one contained directions for dealing with immoral behavior in the community (1 Cor 5:9-11). In 2 Corinthians Paul again refers to a letter sent to the community. "For I wrote you out of much distress and anguish of heart and with many tears, not to cause you pain, but to let you know the abundant love that I have for you" (2 Cor 2:4). This comment refers to a letter of tears and anguish (2 Cor 7:8.12) that may be either 2 Corinthians 10-13 or another lost letter. The apostle also refers to how he writes: "For we write you nothing other than what you can read and also understand" (2 Cor 1:13). Communication is important to Paul, and he attempts to convey his message with clarity. He also knows that his written words are sometimes strong but seems to prefer this approach with the community (2 Cor 10:10).

Within these letters, we also read of Paul's past and proposed visits to this church. In addition to his founding visit when he first proclaimed the Gospel in Corinth, Paul speaks about his desire to visit again, to spend some time with them, and then to go on to Jerusalem (1 Cor 16:3-5). Paul makes a second painful visit (2 Cor 2:1-2), and still anticipates a third visit to this church (2 Cor 12:14). In between visits he has contacts with the church through Timothy, Titus, and messengers from Corinth (1 Cor 1:11; 4:17; 16:10.17-18; 2 Cor 7:6-7; 8:16-19; 12:18). Paul also receives letters from the church (1 Cor 7:1). This data can help us to piece together the development of the correspondence.

The Development of the Corinthian Correspondence

Within 1 and 2 Corinthians we can identify four or five letters written by the apostle Paul to the church in Corinth. The following tables visually represent two of the ways to understand and organize the data given us in the biblical text.

TABLE 4: FOUR LETTERS OF PAUL TO CORINTHIANS

NUMBER OF LETTERS	REFERENCE	DATE	DESCRIPTION OF LETTER
A = 1	1 Cor 5:9	51-54 (?)	Lost Letter
B = 2	1 Cor 16:17-18	(?)53-54	(our) 1 Cor
C = 3	2 Cor 2:3-4.9; 7:8.12	55	2 Cor 10-13 Tearful Letter
D = 4		56(?)	2 Cor 1-9 Letter of Reconciliation

TABLE 5: FIVE LETTERS OF PAUL TO THE CORINTHIANS

NUMBER OF LETTERS	REFERENCE	DATE	DESCRIPTION OF LETTER
A = 1	1 Cor 5:9	51-54(?)	Lost Letter
B = 2	1 Cor 16:17-18	(?)53-54	(our) 1 Cor
C = 3	2 Cor 2:3-4.9; 7:8.12	54-55	Lost Tearful Letter
D = 4		55	2 Cor 1-9 Letter of Reconciliation
E = 5		56	2 Cor 10-13 Angry Letter

While both understandings of the development of these letters have scholarly support, we assume five letters to the

Corinthians in this book. This theory has more convincing arguments for the lost "Sorrowful" letter, and it also coincides with the order in the scripture text (Barrett, *2 Corinthians*, 5-21; Furnish 35-41). The order is important for the reader since it conveys something of the development of the relationship between Paul and the Corinthian church. Either the last recorded encounter is one of reconciliation (Table 4), or the harsh words of Paul convey the progressive deterioration of ties between apostolic founder and church (Table 5). We can now turn to each of the letters as we have them in the Scriptures.

Overview of the Content

1 Corinthians

After Paul preached the Gospel in Corinth during his founding visit, he traveled on to Ephesus, wrote back to the community, and, in turn, received oral and written communication from Corinth. Paul's response to verbal reports and written questions is this practical letter, which gives us a fair picture of issues of interest to this community. In fact, it is important to keep in mind that Paul writes about matters that concern the community, and the content of the letter, as we have it, is in large measure determined by the Christians in Corinth.

Paul responds directly and decisively to verbal reports. He speaks with authority, condemns the past behavior of the community, and challenges those who err (1 Cor 6:5-12). He refers to his former teaching, or that of the coworkers, when he uses the phrase "Do you not know...?" (1 Cor 6:15). News from Corinth and Paul's reaction to it constitutes most of the early part of this letter (1 Cor 1:10-6:20).

However, a major portion of the correspondence is a response to the questions raised by this Christian community. A phrase "now concerning" or, more explicitly, "now concerning the matters about which you wrote" indicates Corinthian questions and issues (1 Cor 7:1). Paul answers these concerns in a careful and detailed manner, as we will see in the following sections. It is possible to reconstruct the letter the Corinthians sent to Paul from material of this kind in the text and from quotes that Paul extracts from their letter to him (1 Cor 6:12.13; 7:1; 8:1.5.8; 11:2) (Hurd 63-68).

No one doubts that 1 Corinthians is a single letter written by Paul. Underlying its practicality is a balanced theology and principles for Christian behavior. Ideas on true wisdom, the Lord's Supper, unity of the body of Christ, spiritual gifts, Christian love, and resurrection provide a comprehensive theological grounding for the community. We also see problems of immorality, interest in lifestyles such as marriage and celibacy, specific issues such as food offered to idols, emphasis on distinctions between women and men, and the impact of social practice on worship in the early church. Paul and the Corinthians seem to disagree on certain matters, a point that accounts for the level of intensity and interest in the letter.

This letter indicates that Paul is willing to grow with the community, challenge them, respond to their inquiries, reaffirm his past teaching, and suggest further ideas. He offers us a model as we respond to issues in our communities. Likewise, he sees worship as integral to life and reflective of deeper attitudes and practices in the congregation. This connection between life and worship is essential to celebrations of the community. Assisting a community in its development, challenging its perspective, and offering a fuller understanding of what it means to be church are Paul's tasks and mission, and ours as well. Being in touch with the present moment and discerning the real issues at stake are what ministry is all about for the apostle and for us. Some would say that Paul was reasonably effective in 1 Corinthians, since we hear nothing of the factions, of Apollos, or of the specific problems of chapters 7-15 in 2 Corinthians (Meeks 118; Barrett, *2 Corinthians*, 6).

2 Corinthians 1-9

Our 2 Corinthians, "the most extraordinary letter of the New Testament" (Murphy-O'Connor, "Coauthorship," 579), is a composite letter that is very personal and perplexing. The human emotion of Paul fills its pages, and its composition places difficulties in the path of the contemporary reader. Realizing the changed situation between 1 Corinthians (Letter B) and 2 Corinthians 1-9 (Letter D) helps us to better understand the material and Paul's passionate response to the church. Factions now become opposition to the apostle; the difficulties, stemming from his painful visit and his strong letter, cause tears and anguish for the community and himself. This letter attempts to reconcile Paul and the Corinthians and to bring both to a new level of understanding. Within its pages we see the closest thing to an apology by Paul as he mentions his regret in provoking their response to his previous letter (2 Cor 7:8). The tone and content is conciliatory yet realistically challenging. In the section on the ministry of reconciliation, Paul reveals his attitude toward his role as servant and disciple and his attempt to maintain a good relationship with the community (2 Cor 5:17-19). Words of consolation, of respect for God's work in the community, of the meaning of affliction, of confidence in the outcome of their mutual struggle, of affection, pleading and rejoicing, fill the pages of this moving letter. The practicalities of a collection and proposed visits indicate the future plans of Paul and the coworkers.

Although this letter addresses a particular situation in a specific church, it has enduring value and provides an inspiring example of the apostle's commitment to the community (Fallon 10). Paul's sensitivity and concern allows him to reach out to the community, as does ours, in difficult situations of ministry. In addition, he seems to put problems into a larger perspective, reminding the community of the reality of the new creation and the hope of future glory. While we may not correspond with our communities as Paul did, liturgical celebrations allow us to taste something of the fullness of life and to see reality from the vantage point of hope. Most revealing in this letter is Paul's sense of heartfelt reconciliation despite grave difficulties in the recent past—its tone and spirit is a model for celebrations of reconciliation in our faith communities.

2 Corinthians 10-13

This harsh or severe letter (Letter E) represents a rapidly deteriorating situation in the Corinthian church that we can deduce from the correspondence. Earlier problems regarding factions, teaching, and practice (1 Corinthians) give way to opposition to Paul's ministry and to confrontational attitudes. We can almost taste the anxiety and intensity of this phase of the relationship between Paul and the Corinthian church. Paul counters charges against him, attacks those who oppose him, and boasts about his apostolic credentials. This letter seems to be written in anger rather than in sorrow (Furnish 37-38), and it reflects one of the great crises of Paul's career. The underlying issue may be Paul himself, but little doubt remains about the intensity of the apostle's feelings and concerns. Read in a positive way, 2 Corinthians 10-13 identifies the qualities and characteristics of authentic ministry as enumerated and exemplified by Paul.

The tone and content of this letter differ from 2 Corinthians 1-9. Paul's uses the technique of boasting in what some commentators call "The Fool's Speech." He places his apostleship, his ministry, and his Gospel above that of his opponents. He recalls aspects of his background and difficulties in his ministry to a fault. He speaks of peak religious experiences to challenge the claims of the opposition, but the reader is left breathless and wondering. What is his purpose? Why does he protest so much? He anticipates another visit to the community and recalls the crucified Lord, the model for his ministry. He then appeals to the community to "Put things in order, listen to my appeal, agree with one another, live in peace; and the God of love and peace will be with you" (2 Cor 13:11).

While most of us would shrink from writing such a severe letter and hope that our relationship to the communities we serve would never deteriorate to this point, we can take heart that our beginnings as church were not as idealistic and trouble free as some people would like to imagine. The Corinthian letters represent the real difficulties of living in a period of transition, and we can identify with the struggles they faced in the process of change. Paul and the church bring the mutual experience that provoked the writing of 2 Corinthians 10-13 to its own liturgical celebrations, a poignant reminder that we often do the same. Yet, a reason for Christian hope lies within the theological framework of the entire correspondence with Corinth. We must uncover this virtue, in order to give the world and ourselves new reasons to live and reasons to hope, as the Vatican Council challenges us (*Church in the Modern World* 31).

Factions and Opposition in the Corinthian Church

In the three letters to Corinth, preserved for us in the New Testament, we discover factions in the community and opposition to Paul. Corinth itself had a history of factions and so their presence within the Christian community is not surprising. "Nothing was more characteristic of the Corinthian church than its tendency to division" (Barrett, *2 Corinthians*, 36). Within 1 Corinthians we see evidence of disruption that is internal to the community, affecting its unity as the body of Christ. "For it has been reported to me by Chloe's people that there are quarrels among you, my brothers and sisters. What I mean is that each of you says, 'I belong to Paul,' or 'I belong to Apollos,' or 'I belong to Cephas,' or 'I belong to Christ'" (1 Cor 1:11-12). The difficulty appears to be on the level of the followers, primarily those of Paul and Apollos (1 Cor 1:12; 3:2-4.22; 4:6), who identify with different qualities in the minister and different theological emphases. Apollos, known for his eloquence, had great success in Corinth and probably represented to his followers a theology of exaltation with its emphasis on wisdom and spiritual gifts. Paul had considerably less appeal since he presented his message in ordinary speech, challenged worldly wisdom and the spiritual gifts exalted by the community, and emphasized the cross of Christ. These factions reflect the immaturity of the Corinthians (1 Cor 3:1; 14:20) and some conflict between the church its founder, Paul. Most commentators agree no rivalry existed between Paul and Apollos although some of the teaching that the Corinthians found appealing may be linked to Apollos.

Paul views the Corinthians as not living up to their potential and later puts a positive spin on the existence of factions in the community. "Indeed, there have to be factions among you, for only so will it become clear who among you are genuine" (1 Cor 11:19). This comment occurs within the context of the divisions in the Christian assembly (1 Cor 11:17-18). Paul registers concern that when the community celebrates the Lord's Supper, they reflect the social stratification of Corinth rather than the unity of the church. That this community had to strive for unity encourages us as local communities and a universal church. That the celebration of Eucharist reflected the quality of community life speaks to our liturgical ministry, which must include both preparation for the celebration and community formation.

The Corinthian letters document that Paul experiences opposition to himself, his ideas, and his ministry. Paul states: "But with me it is a very small thing that I should be judged by you or by any human court...do not pronounce judgment before the time, before the Lord comes" (1 Cor 4:3.5). With their different views on wisdom and judgment, contention develops between Paul and the community (1 Cor 1:17-21). The Corinthians also emphasize the wonders of spiritual gifts (1 Cor 14:18.22) and see little need for resurrection of the body (1 Cor 15:4.12) (Roetzel, "Dying," 7). Paul deals with such enthusiasts and clarifies the importance of his teaching: "Whether then it was I or they, so we proclaim and so you have come to believe" (1 Cor 15:11).

Between 1 and 2 Corinthians, opposition changes from internal dissension to external strife. Paul speaks strongly: "For such boasters are false apostles, deceitful workers, disguising themselves as apostles of Christ" (2 Cor 11:13). He also defends himself and his ministry: "I think that I am not in the least inferior to these super-apostles" (2 Cor 11:5). Underlying these comments is a radically different view of apostleship and ministry, suggesting different types of missionaries in Corinth (Theissen 40). Understanding the opposition's accusations of weakness, inconsistency, and fraud enables us to put Paul's personal response in perspective. He denies charges and criticizes his opponents (2 Cor 3:1; 5:12; 10:12.18). His self-commendation in 2 Corinthians 11-12 indicates his strong personal feeling against the "false apostles" (2 Cor 11:13) and identifies the qualities he associates with the true minister of the Gospel. In addition, the fact that the Corinthians do not seem to boast of Paul to rival missionaries (2 Cor 5:12) affects Paul in his work with the church.

Who are the opponents in 2 Corinthians? Many scholarly discussions focus on their identity and two strong possibilities emerge, that of Jewish Christians of Palestinian origin who observed the law and Hellenistic-Jewish itinerant preachers who possessed the Spirit (Furnish 48-54; Murphy-O'Connor, *2 Corinthians*, 12-15; Barrett, *2 Corinthians*,

28-30). Many see the false apostles or super apostles as the same group and identify them as Jewish Christians who claim authority in the community (2 Cor 11:22). They have a charismatic quality that strengthens their appeal in a Hellenistic environment and, as representatives from the Jerusalem church, they do not accept Paul's apostolic authority (Barrett, *2 Corinthians*, 6-7.30). Rather than single missionaries, these opponents seem to be representative of a group that may indicate the majority position in Corinth (Georgi, *Opponents*, 174). Although no apparent consensus exists regarding the identity of the opposition group in Corinth, their influence is evident in the letters.

The power of a group to sway the Corinthian community is apparent not only in the early church, but also within our own Christian communities. The message of a rival group is, at times, strikingly similar to our own understanding, a fact that some identify in Paul's experience of opposition in Corinth (Georgi 365). Our awareness of the existence of conflict in this church enables us to set an appropriate context for some of the difficult liturgical readings we have from the Corinthian letters.

Opposition groups, with their challenges, allow Christians of every period to clarify their own understanding of theology and ministry. The existence of several letters containing a record of the issues and the opposition in Corinth contributes to our understanding of the growth of the early church. In addition, we see in the pages of 1 and 2 Corinthians how a leader and a community handle crisis, deal with dissent, settle disagreements, reestablish authority, and foster community growth. Paul faces opposition, and whether he succeeds or fails in his approach is not as important as his attitude, manner, conviction, and motivation. If we meet failure nobly, the results in our own lives will not differ from success.

Paul the Writer

Purpose of the Letters

Paul's letters are conversations with the community that arise out of unique situations and stand as a substitute for his apostolic presence. Following on Paul's initial preaching and teaching, he draws on a different form of communication and writes as a seasoned missionary. The letter form itself is an indicator of what Paul intends. Its components include an opening *salutation, thanksgiving* for the faith of the community, a main section or *body* that contains theology appropriate to community concerns, a series of *exhortations* or challenges to the community that are often culturally conditioned, and a *closing* that includes greetings and travel plans. It is of interest that Paul first offers thanks to God for the community, then provides a basis for understanding the essence of the Gospel message, and lastly identifies some practical implications for Christian life. This progression from affirmation to theological reflection to everyday examples offers us an outline for effective homilies. It creates a balance between instruction and challenge that usually works well.

Paul's topics and themes in his letters interest the community and contribute to its growth. He allows the dynamics of the church's situation to determine the letter's tone and pace, as should be the case in preaching the word. Likewise, Paul builds on previous teaching and a personal relationship with the community in his correspondence, factors in pastoral effectiveness today.

In 1 Corinthians, Paul brings "the gospel to bear in the marketplace" (Fee 16). He deals with the situation, issues, and questions of the community (11 different ones emerge), anticipates problems, and attempts to effect change by offering his understanding of the Gospel.

In 2 Corinthians 1-9, Paul assures the community of his concerns and sets a context for reconciliation. He also seeks to strengthen the commitment of the Corinthians to his apostolic ministry and to the Gospel.

In 2 Corinthians 10-13, Paul defends himself and his apostleship, challenging the attitudes of those who oppose him and his message.

While the focus of each letter and its purpose differs, Paul's commitment to the community comes through in the text and its dialogue. The Corinthians, too, are eager to grow in faith, and the difficulties both need to address come from the energy and intensity on the part of both minister and church. Identifying a focus for our liturgical celebrations enables us to shape the experience as Paul shaped his written correspondence. As we clarify our purpose, from the readings in the liturgical cycle and the interests of the community, we contribute to the development of a Christian consciousness, as did the apostle to the Gentiles.

Style of Writing

Understanding a first-century document is difficult because the style of writing is so different than our own. Sometimes we feel strangely removed from Paul; at other times, when we can identify with the material, we feel comfortably engaged in the dialogue. In the letters to the Corinthians we can identify stylistic characteristics, use of material, and ways of argumentation that allow us to enter into the Greco-Roman literary world and, thus in turn, to grasp the full significance of Paul's meaning in the biblical text. Examining the language, terminology, and structure of 1 and 2 Corinthians can facilitate our preparation of the scriptural readings for liturgy, as well as offering explanations for the difficult images and teachings we encounter within the context of liturgical celebrations.

In Corinthians Paul uses the Jewish Scriptures with explanatory commentary or interpretive additions to the text. These Scriptures, and his contrast of Adam and Christ, form the basis of Paul's theological understanding of the transformational significance of Christ's resurrection (1 Cor 15). Our biblical texts belong to a patriarchal culture that envisions reality from the vantage point of the male. Our awareness of this background enables us to understand the prevalence of male and hierarchical images. Paul's teaching on marriage and his assessment of roles in the Christian assembly that seem so strange to us (1 Cor 7 and 11) also reflect the influences of patriarchy and his own conflict between social norms and the Gospel message.

Paul is creative and original in his thinking as he describes communal unity in terms of the body of Christ (1 Cor 12). At times, inconsistencies or contradictions occur in Paul's statements, and some scholars attribute these to later editorial insertions into the text. The passage on women's roles in the assembly (1 Cor 14:33-36), which stands at odds with Paul's earlier comment (1 Cor 11:5), is an example.

Use of Language

Language is the vehicle Paul uses to preach the Gospel and convey its impact on Christian life. The *imagery* Paul uses in his letters reflects his world and Corinthian interests, with many more references to urban rather than rural life. Paul envisions believers as athletes in pursuit of the prize or goal, a recognizable image from the Isthmian games (1 Cor 9:24-27). Christians are God's temple and building, a picture from Corinth itself with its temples to gods and goddesses and its grand urban environment (1 Cor 3:16-17; 2 Cor 5:1). Triumphant processions (2 Cor 2:14), musical instruments (1 Cor 13:1; 14:7-8.10-11; 15:52), clay jars and treasures (2 Cor 4:7), peddlers (2 Cor 2:17), earthly tents (2 Cor 5:1.4), and clothing (2 Cor 5:2.4) are vivid images from life in this great city. Paul also speaks of war, with references to strongholds, captives, weapons of warfare, and destruction, reminding us of the conquests of the period (2 Cor 10:4-13). Interest in heavenly bodies and the glory of the sun, moon, and stars indicate astrological and apocalyptic interests in Corinth and allow for dramatic portrayals of the resurrection and parousia (1 Cor 15:40-41). References to fields, seeds, wheat, grain, sowing, and planting remind the Corinthians of the process of growth in faith. Paul's language reflects the surrounding areas and its fruits in the marketplace (1 Cor 3:6-8; 15:37; 2 Cor 10:13).

Paul teaches the Corinthian church by using familiar pictures and impressions from their daily life. We also draw on images related to life for our educational and liturgical instruction. While these may differ from those in the biblical text, our examples convey meaning, just as Paul's did.

The apostle develops simple images into *metaphors* for his theological insights. Thus, Paul's use of the earthly tent and heavenly house (2 Cor 5:1-5) and the sweet fragrances, bad odors, and triumphal procession, expand into metaphors of resurrection (2 Cor 2:14-17). Metaphors sometimes become *symbols* that evoke a response in people of faith, such as the symbol of the cross for Christians today. Some symbols evolve into models that allow us to critique and explore a fuller meaning of the message, such as the "new creation" and "body of Christ" to describe the community of believers (H. Doohan, *Vision*, 137-138). Sensitivity to powerful symbols for the community is part of our liturgical ministry, and it implies knowing the interests of people in our churches. An Alaskan community told us how it was more important that all rowers pull together, than it was to have a captain for the boat to move forward. "If we don't row together, the captain goes nowhere." What potential for a model of church and for collaborative government in that area!

While Paul uses language in a positive way to convey his understanding of theology, church, and Christian life, he also relies on negative statements and *contrast* to startle his audience and to invite them to critique their own ideas. The opening section of 1 Corinthians uses many negative participles (1:14-3:4), and the reader knows that Paul places importance on the opposite quality. The apostle uses antithesis, with its vivid contrasts, to make a dramatic theological point (2 Cor 6:9-10), paradox to provide glimpses of the radical implications of Gospel (1 Cor 1:23-25), rhetorical questions to engage the thought of the reader (1 Cor 10:29-30), sarcasm and irony to challenge his opponents and to put their charges in perspective (2 Cor 10-13). Paul awakens his audience's attention with his striking contrasts, and he produces similar effects with his use of apocalyptic descriptions. These dramatic images prevail in the early letters of Paul when he speaks of the second coming and the resurrection (1 Thess 4:16; 1 Cor 15:23-28).

Some of Paul's statements and colorful techniques can be misunderstood in other cultures, as is often the case when we hear such passages in liturgical readings. Knowing what, how, and why Paul chooses particular language or approach in his letters allows us to set a context for interpretation for our congregation.

Literary Techniques

Paul incorporates ideas from the Corinthian community and traditions of the early church into the letters he writes. Within the Corinthian correspondence, Paul refers to his previous teaching or to important instruction when he uses the formula, "I do not want you to be ignorant" (1 Cor 10:1-13; 12:1; 2 Cor 1:8). In 1 Corinthians he explicitly recalls the words of the Lord (7:10; 9:14; 11:23-26; 14:37). His inclusion of the eucharistic words of Jesus in chapter 11 is the earliest account we have, predating Mark's Gospel by approximately fifteen years. Corinthian *slogans*, known by Paul, identify the important maxims of the community that he challenged (1 Cor 8:4; 6:12; 10:23). Paul anchors his thought in his audience's world, and his use of their slogans allows us to see how his teaching develops. He also quotes extensively from the Corinthians' letter to him (1 Cor 1:12; 2:15; 6:12-13; 7:1; 8:1.4.8; 10:23; 11:2; 15:12), again indicating the community's perspective as well as his own reflection on their views. The apostle occasionally preserves confessional or *kerygmatic* statements (1 Cor 15:3-7) that offer glimpses into the beliefs of the early church.

Most interesting and, perhaps, foreign to us is Paul's use of *rhetoric* that indicates his ability to use a refined form of discourse to persuade his readers. The arguments are sophisticated and complex (Wire, chapter 2) but adapted by the apostle to deal with concerns and to refine his theology (1 Cor 9). He also utilizes *diatribe*, or a lively argument with an imaginary opponent, to clarify his ideas for the church. These approaches appeal to his audience who know the logic of debate from the rhetorical discourse heard in the forums of Corinth. When we read the text, we must often put together the pieces of the puzzle, a step omitted by the Corinthians who were familiar with rules of rhetoric (1 Cor 12:31; 13:3). Paul mastered this technique and felt assured in his usage. He understood the place of audience reaction and, like speakers or writers of the day, could engage the church in judgment, deliberation, or the pure intellectual enjoyment of the argument (Florenza, "1 Corinthians," 390).

In the Corinthian letters, Paul attempts to persuade Christians to take appropriate action or to change their position.

These various components of Paul's writing style make his letters interesting to read and challenging to interpret. Some of the more intricate techniques speak to the sophistication of the Corinthians and the quality of their life. As preachers of the word, we have the power to influence and to persuade our congregations. How we utilize this ability in our liturgical celebrations may differ from Paul's approach, but we must realize the opportunity and the responsibility that is ours.

Terminology

Paul conveys his understanding of the human person, union with Christ, and view of the world in expressions and phrases that have specific connotations for his audience. For example, he views the human person as an integrated whole, even though he uses language such as "flesh" and "spirit," "body" and "mind," "spiritual" and "unspiritual." Paul's use of dualism or contrast makes a theological point since he regards the individual and humankind as a unity. Understanding underlying thought patterns is important for us so that we can accurately interpret these first century documents for our audiences.

More specifically, the apostle uses "body" (*soma*) to convey the idea of the person, the self, the living being with all his or her potential. This person can be under the sway of sin and death or under the power of the Lord (1 Cor 6:13). Paul's use of "flesh" (*sarx*) for the physical body or humanity subject to weakness and frailty indicates differentiation from God. Moreover, "flesh" and "sinful flesh" need not coincide in biblical thought. Rather, "flesh" indicates our transitory existence and our need of transformation (Fitzmyer, *Theology*, 61; Ellis, "Soma," 134; Ridderbos 65). This meaning is important to adequately examine Paul's sexual ethics (1 Cor 1-7), the Lord's Supper (10-11), gifts of ministry (12), and resurrection theology (15)—some of the most misinterpreted texts in the New Testament (Ellis, "Soma," 132).

Use of "spirit" (*pneuma*) indicates the human spirit open to receive the spirit of God. This term conveys human consciousness, intelligence, and understanding along with "soul" (*psyche*), a closely related term. Unlike our understanding, "soul" is more "material" than "spiritual" in Paul's time. "Mind" (*nous*) and "heart" (*kardia*) have similar meaning, indicating vision, intelligent understanding, purpose, and decision.

Paul understands that the Corinthian Christians live in the world, the embodiment of their concerns, and they attempt to bring the transformational power of Christ to bear on all their efforts. The most insightful terminology Paul uses to indicate Christian incorporation into Christ are the simple phrases "through" (*dia*), "into" (*eis*), "with" (*syn*), and "in" (*en*) Christ. Theological meaning fills these simple expressions for they respectively signify Christ as mediator of God's action, our movement toward Christ in baptism, our association with him in suffering and glory, and our intimate union with the Lord. A most powerful insight for Paul is that the Christian is in Christ, that is, participating in Christ's life, drawing on his abiding presence and power, and living in constant union with the Lord. When we grasp his meaning in such phrases, we can better understand Paul's extraordinary challenges to the Corinthian church. Reminding our congregations of their true identity in Christ, as the apostle did, forms a basis for the challenges we offer in our homilies and educational offerings.

Language, thought patterns, and simple expressions contribute to the development of themes and theology in 1 and 2 Corinthians. Whether Paul speaks about unity, the body of Christ, resurrection, equality, or freedom, we need a frame of reference to understand his meaning.

Outline and Structure of the Corinthian Letters

The following outlines of Paul's letters to the Corinthians focus on aspects of liturgical celebration and Christian ministry. As we explore some of the theology, issues, and liturgical interests in the later chapters of the book, these outlines will enable us to see, at a glance, the placement of material under discussion. Likewise, we will be able to readily identify the context for scriptural readings used in our celebrations and so facilitate our liturgical preparation.

TABLE 6: OUTLINE AND STRUCTURE OF THE LETTERS

1 CORINTHIANS (LETTER B)	
Celebration of Thanks	
1:1-3	Introduction and greeting
1:4-9	Thanksgiving
Divisions in the Community and Paul's Preaching	
Celebration of True Wisdom	
1:10-17	Presence of factions in the community
1:18-31	Wisdom of God
2:1-16	Paul's preaching
3:1-9	Problems in the community
3:10-4:21	Paul's ministry in the church
Celebration of the Body	
5:1-13	Dealing with immorality
6:1-11	Lawsuits and judgment
6:12-20	Approaches to ethical issues
Reply to Corinthian Questions	
Celebration of Lifestyles	
7:1-9	Concerning relations in marriage
7:10-16	Marriage and divorce
7:17-24	Changes in social status
7:25-40	Paul's teaching on relationships
Celebration of Worship in Corinth	
8:1-13	Concerning food to idols
9:1-10:22	Paul's freedom as an apostle
10:23-11:1	Paul's teaching for the community

Celebration of Christian Worship	
11:2-16	Roles and behavior in the Christian assembly
11:17-22	Situation in Corinth
11:23-26	The Lord's Supper
11:27-34	Paul's teaching for the church
Celebration of Community	
12:1-31	Spiritual gifts and the body of Christ
13:1-13	Christian love
14:1-40	Paul's teaching on spiritual gifts and order
Celebration of Fullness of Life	
15:1-11	Christian belief
15:12-19	Corinthian's problem
15:20-50	Paul's teaching on resurrection
15:51-58	Final transformation in Christ
Celebration of Church Unity	
16:1-4	Collection
16:5-18	Visits and concluding comments
16:19-24	Final greetings
2 CORINTHIANS 1-9 (LETTER D)	
1:1-2	Greetings
1:3-11	Thanksgiving
Paul, Minister of the Gospel	
1:12-14	Paul's sincerity
1:15-2:13	Visits and concerns
Authentic Christian Ministry	
2:14-3:6	Understanding and experience of ministry

3:7-4:6	Contrasts in ministry
4:7-5:10	Trials and hopes of the minister
5:11-21	Reconciliation and the new creation
6:1-10	Paradox of Christian ministry
6:11-7:16	Corinthian situation and Paul's ministry
Mutual Responsibility	
8:1-24	Collection for the poor in Jerusalem
9:1-15	Paul's challenge to generosity
2 CORINTHIANS 10-13 (LETTER E)	
Qualities of Christian Ministry	
10:1-18	Paul's defense of his apostleship
11:1 12:13	Foolishness of the apostle
12:14-13:10	Visits and warning
13:11-13	Final comments and greetings

Witness to Growth in the Corinthian Correspondence

Paul's letters to the Corinthians reveal growth and change in the relationship between founder and community. We see how both parties deal with change and crises, personal pain and challenge, misunderstanding and opposition. In the early stages of Paul's relationship with the church, he maintains a spirit that allows the Corinthians to ask the important questions contained in 1 Corinthians (Letter B). While factions and problems emerge in the community, he writes letters and sends emissaries to clarify the issues at stake. Given the Corinthians' background and environment, we expect them to explore new ideas, challenge teaching, and question authority.

When the relationship between Paul and the community continues to deteriorate, as we read in our 2 Corinthians (Letters D and E), we witness strong feelings, powerful opposition, frequent misunderstanding, and passionate responses. That such problems find their way into our Scriptures allows us to understand, first hand, the struggles of the early Christian community and to form a realistic view of the beginnings of our church. We can also view the responses and strategies of Paul in dealing with issues and assess their appropriateness in our own ministerial situations.

Paul and the community grow at different rates in their understanding of the Gospel. Sometimes the apostle is ahead of the church, at other times, the community surpasses its founder in its ideas and practice. For example, Paul understands the significance of the cross of Christ, while the Corinthians take women's equality in the church to its logical conclusions in liturgical celebrations and lifestyles. This maturing of thought and practice allows for clarification of the Gospel and for refinement of Christian principles in a Gentile environment. This process continues to our day as we attempt to clarify, refine, and reinterpret the biblical message for communities that differ culturally, economically, and religiously from their ancestors.

The apostle Paul offers us a variety of options for addressing difficult situations. He responds to reports about factions with strength and conviction, and he attempts to understand the Corinthian's need to emulate their apostles and validate their understanding of wisdom. He answers their questions carefully and cleverly, convinced that they will follow his advice. An identifiable theological framework underlying his responses allows the Corinthians, and ourselves, to come to appropriate conclusions as believers. Paul pays attention to these followers, although he also alienates some of them.

When Paul deals with opposition, as in 2 Corinthians, he confronts opponents and challenges their ideas. He uses unusual techniques, such as boasting, to present alternative values. Writing a harsh letter or seeking reconciliation is not beyond the very human Paul that emerges in this letter. While no one can doubt that Paul has the community's benefit at heart, he emotionally responds to the Corinthian church in ways that are puzzling and overly dramatic to contemporary readers. As a Christian minister, Paul addresses an overwhelmingly difficult situation in this community in a variety of ways. From a distance, through letters, and firsthand, by visits, he struggles to preserve his integrity and that of the Gospel he preaches. The New Testament rarely offers such a view of the dynamics at work in the early church.

Interesting, as well, is the witness of the Corinthian correspondence to the implications of belief. Faith and life form an integrated whole; the Gospel impacts the marketplace. Within our liturgical celebrations, we attempt to correlate these realities in preaching and through ritual. Corinth's issues may not be ours, but the areas of concern in our church and world must be incorporated in our celebrations of faith and worship.

The biblical text comes to us under the cultural nuances of the first century, which includes patriarchy. Feminist biblical scholars attempt to recover and reconstruct the text to lessen its oppressive features and unfold its liberating message. Language has the power to conceal and to reveal, and so attempts to understand the thought and reality behind the words of the text are essential. These letters contain marvelous testimony to women's roles in the community and to their dedicated response to the Gospel. As we examine texts such as 1 Corinthians 7,11,14 in the upcoming chapters, we should be aware that limiting the inclusion of women in the Scriptures or their roles in the early church was a by-product of the times. But, it is no justification for their exclusion today. How different our understanding of Christianity would be if we had a framework other than patriarchy operative in the biblical period.

These letters to the Corinthians offer hope to churches living through critical and transitional periods. Questioning by the Christian community, poignant and practical responses by the apostle, obvious changes in relationship, and the need for mutual reconciliation and respect echo the experience of many churches today. When we proclaim these readings in our liturgical celebrations, let us be aware of the underlying struggles for an authentic response to the Gospel that was theirs. This insight will enable us to embrace the challenges inherent in a reinterpretation of the Gospel message today.

For Personal and Group Reflection

1. The apostle Paul continued to grow in his relationship with the Corinthian church through letters and visits. Describe the various and creative ways you develop relationships in your exercise of ministry.

2. The Corinthian letters can be read in two different ways, as suggested in Tables 1 & 2. In both approaches, Paul's relationship with the community deteriorated. How do you deal with misunderstanding and anger in the exercise of ministry?

3. Paul responded to verbal reports and to written questions raised by the Corinthian community. What are concerns and questions of the community you serve?

4. Which aspects of the Corinthian correspondence do you think are pastorally significant for you in your ministry?

5. Paul faced opposition in his work with the community. How would you describe opposition and factions in the local church? How do you facilitate community growth in these situations?

6. Paul used a style of writing and terminology that is sometimes foreign to the contemporary reader. Which clarifications in the these sections helped you to better understand Paul and his letters?

7. In pastoral settings we, like Paul, often need to translate religious concepts for people who have little understanding of the

tradition. How do you meet this challenge in your ministry?

8. Paul's letters to the Corinthians contained a series of issues, questions, and perspectives on ministry geared to this early Christian community. From the outline of the letters, which seem to address your situation? Which seem totally foreign? Why?

9. The Corinthian letters reflect growth and change in Paul and the community. How has your community changed in the last two years? How do you deal with varying levels of growth in the congregation?

10. Personal relationships seem to be important in faith communities, particularly in times of transition. How do interpersonal relations in your community affect your ability to minister in the Lord's name?

Chapter 3

Paul's Gospel

The Corinthian correspondence is among the earliest written testimony to the beliefs of the church in its formative stages of development. While still under the umbrella of Judaism, Christians clarified their understanding of the Lord in relation to their Jewish roots by reexamining its Scriptures, religious rites, and rituals. An expansive missionary movement quickly brought the Gospel to many Gentile communities living in a largely Hellenistic environment. Paul's and the coworkers' task was to proclaim the Gospel to this audience, and this, of necessity, included some adaptation of the original message. Religious concepts, language, and experience differed for these Hellenistic Gentile groups, and letters, like those sent to Corinth, contain material that is both handed on and interpreted.

In our examination of the origin and transmission of the Gospel, we will see how Paul utilizes the tradition and incorporates into his preaching insights from his own conversion. The kerygma within the Corinthian letters reflects essential elements in the proclamation of faith by early Christians. As the faith of these communities grew under the guidance of the Spirit, theological insights also developed. The Corinthian correspondence allows us to witness this process of clarifying beliefs. Since situation determines the form and provides the context for Paul's theological reflections, he often focuses 1 and 2 Corinthians as a response to dissent and opposition. Although Paul's theology comes to us piecemeal, intertwined in Corinthian issues, these letters still present within their pages a comprehensive Christian understanding of God, Jesus, and the Spirit.

Later writers and commentators interpret and systematize Paul's theology, but we can examine his insights as the first readers would have received them, embedded in the text. We undoubtedly recognize the faith professed by the Corinthian Christians as we read the letters, and identify with their struggles to identify the practical implications of belief for daily life. Likewise, Paul's proclamation of the Gospel reflects his own faith, just as the word we preach indicates our religious convictions. Central to the Christian Gospel is belief in God's salvific action in Jesus, and Paul bases his many exhortations to the community on this revelation. Theological conviction should also be the basis for the practical suggestions we offer to our congregations today.

Paul's Proclamation of the Gospel

The Origin of the Gospel

In the letters to the Corinthians Paul uses the term "gospel" to describe the person and message of Jesus, the focus of Paul's own ministry, and the essence of Christian belief. The word itself was used in the Jewish Scriptures in a religious sense in conjunction with the reign and power of God (Isa 52:1-7). Greeks and Romans used "gospel" or "good news" to announce a victory and to record events in the lives of significant people. When Paul and other New Testament writers use this term they have in mind the good news of salvation now realized in the person Jesus. The gospel form associated with Matthew, Mark, Luke, and John is a later development in New Testament writings.

The good news of God's work in and through Jesus was originally proclaimed through preaching. Paul's use of the term and his identification of the content of the Gospel is the earliest written record available to us. Even in Paul's case, he was first a preacher of the Word, then a writer. Within our liturgical contexts, we know the importance of proclaiming the Word in Scripture readings and of preaching the good news in homilies that bring the Word of God to life for us. Interaction between the spoken and written Word allows for this continual reinterpretation of the Gospel.

The earliest disciples apprehended God's action in Jesus only through the gift of *faith*. Only after his conversion experience did Paul understand the role of Jesus in salvation or the significance of his death and resurrection. "The Gospel that he received on the Damascus road Paul defined, first of all, Christologically" (Kim 100). Paul's religious experience led to his belief in Jesus. "For we do not proclaim ourselves; we proclaim Jesus Christ as Lord and ourselves as your slaves for Jesus' sake" (2 Cor 4:5). Paul also understood the essence of his mission in the Lord's call. "For Christ did not send me to baptize but to proclaim the gospel, and not with eloquent wisdom, so that the cross of Christ might not be emptied of its power" (1 Cor 1:17). He reminds the Corinthians that he was: "the first to come all the way to you with the good news of Christ" (2 Cor 10:14), and that he was "entrusted with a commission" (1 Cor 9:17). Because of his commissioning by God, Paul senses an urgency to preach the Gospel (2 Cor 2:17; 1 Cor 9:15). The apostle grounds his understanding of the Gospel and his authority to preach, primarily, in God's revelation to him. He reflects on his preaching in the course of his ministry and on the insight he receives from the Spirit of God (1 Cor 2:1-16). However, we also know that Paul receives the Gospel from those who were believers before him.

The Tradition of the Early Church

Paul's gospel and theology develop from the earliest proclamation of the church. He acknowledges what he has received from the Lord and from the apostolic tradition handed on to him (1 Cor 7:10; 9:14; 11:5; 11:23-26; 14:34-37; 15:3-8). In his use of this material, Paul is more concerned about the significance of the word for his community than about the word itself. He is interested in interpretation and adaptation of the tradition. "Paul's originality and creativity are to be found not in his doctrinal architecture but in his hermeneutic" (Beker, *Apostle*, 109). However, Paul also urges respect for the tradition, "I commend you because you remember me in everything and maintain the traditions just as I handed them on to you" (1 Cor 11:2), and he often bases his argument on tradition or custom (1 Cor 11:16; 15:51) (Meeks 124).

The Gospel Message

The preaching of the Gospel reflects a spirit of faith: "But just as we have the same spirit of faith that is in accordance with scripture—'I believed, and so I spoke'—we also believe, and so we speak" (2 Cor 4:13). 1 Corinthians contains elements from the earliest kerygmatic formulas. In his eucharistic account, Paul recalls Christ's death and Christian belief in his second coming. "The Lord Jesus on the night when he was betrayed took a loaf of bread....For as often as you eat this bread and drink the cup, you proclaim the Lord's death until he comes" (1 Cor 11:23.26). Within the chapter on resurrection, we identify further elements of the kerygma: "Christ died for our sins in accordance with the scriptures, and that he was buried, and that he was raised on the third day in accordance with the scriptures..." (1 Cor 15:3-4). These professions of belief concur with the kerygma contained in the speeches of Acts (L. Doohan, *Acts*, 66-67, 97), but Paul expands it into the fuller theology of the letters, presenting it in a new way for the Corinthian church (2 Cor 4:6).

In these letters we also have an early attestation to the preexistence of Christ (1 Cor 8:6), the first insight into the effects of God's justice in the Christian Scriptures (2 Cor 5:21), and the recognition of the new creation in Christ (2 Cor 5:17).

While the essence of the Gospel is fairly comprehensive, Paul tends to draw out its implications for the community (1 Cor 15:1-19). The centrality of the cross of Christ in Paul's preaching is evident throughout Corinthians (1 Cor 1:17). Belief in the crucified Christ affects Paul's testimony and demeanor (1 Cor 2:1-2), and he does not deviate from its proclamation even though the cross is "a stumbling block to Jews and foolishness to Gentiles" (1 Cor 1:23). This understanding of the Gospel is so central to Paul's message that he challenges those who preach and accept "another Jesus" (2 Cor 11:4). While the Gospel message is veiled for some (2 Cor 4:3-4), Paul relates aspects of its mystery to the community (1 Cor 15:51).

Paul is passionate about proclaiming the Gospel because his own faith understanding of Jesus radically changed his life. Likewise, he understands the Gospel as inclusive of all peoples, exemplified in his own mission to the Gentiles. Adaptation of the good news allows Paul to bring the message to various communities while still transmitting its core beliefs (1 Cor 2:13). As we liturgically proclaim the Gospel, we too must be inclusive of all and directly relate the Scripture to our own congregations. As participants in the celebration listen to the Word of God, they hear it from their own frames of reference. It could be beneficial for liturgical leaders to monitor, periodically, how the community understands the biblical text. The reader/listener response to Scripture is as important as understanding the first century language and setting, for both elements are part of biblical interpretation.

Hearing, believing, confessing, and living God's Word is the purpose of Gospel proclamation. Its core truths form the basis of Paul's theological understanding in these letters.

The Development of Paul's Theology

Paul's theology develops from an initial understanding in 1 Thessalonians of Jesus as risen Lord who will come again in glory to his focus on the death and resurrection of Jesus that transforms the lives of believers in 1 and 2 Corinthians and other major letters. Paul's theological perspective develops out of his conversion experience, Pharisaic background, Hellenistic influences, early church tradition, and apostolic ministry. Clearly, the theology within these letters is a result of the interaction of these many aspects of Paul's background, as well as dynamic exchanges between apostle, community leaders, and churches. Imagine Paul struggling with issues of continuity between his Jewish belief and his Christian faith! We see an amazing number of convictions associated with Pharisaic faith in the letters (Patte 117), but we can also identify the radical impact of his new understanding of Christ.

Neither is Paul an ivory tower theologian since he develops his insights and critique during his missionary activities. The situations of his pastoral involvement with their challenges, questions, opposition, and tension stimulate his thinking, deepen his convictions, and refine his understanding. Reading Paul's letters in their chronological order allows us to understand the power and simplicity of belief in the early stages of church life and its later theological refinement.

Doing theology is certainly the ministry of Christian leaders, if we see Paul as our model and guide. Theological reflection that resonates with our congregation needs creative thinkers with pastoral experience. We discover many people with these qualities in liturgical ministry. Their sense of community, tradition, culture, and authentic religious experience allows for a dynamic of theological reflection similar to that of Paul.

Faith is inseparable from the theological insight revealed in 1 and 2 Corinthians. Paul's faith in God's salvific action in Christ affects everything he says and does. "From now on, therefore, we regard no one from a human point of view; even though we once knew Christ from a human point of view, we know him no longer in that way" (2 Cor 5:16). While Paul does not define faith, he is convinced that the gift of faith enlightens believers and leads to responsible action (1 Cor 4:7; 2 Cor 5:7). This faith incorporates the entire Gospel, for *"faith is nothing other than holding to a system of convictions or, better, being held by a system of convictions"* (Patte 11).

The Corinthian correspondence contains theology interwoven in the issues and reflections that Paul offers the church. While it is difficult to uncover a coherent center of Paul's theology (Beker, *Heirs*, 20-21) and commentators differ in their assessment (see Plevnik 464), we can identify some key theological components such as an understanding of Christ (Christology), salvation (soteriology), church (ecclesiology), end times (eschatology), and Christian life. Paul's convictions regarding freedom, equality, and community also contribute to the way he deals with the actual issues and questions of the Corinthian church. These recurring insights stem from his understanding of the Gospel, have an impact on his theological development, and provide a foundation for understanding his practical approach to community concerns.

Key Theological Insights in the Corinthian Letters

Reading the Corinthian correspondence often leaves the contemporary Christian wondering about the importance of its issues and the validity of Paul's practical advice to the community. However, no reader would doubt the strength of Paul's and the Corinthians' convictions! Their faith empowers them, and their faith matures in depth and breadth. 1 and 2 Corinthians contain the kernel of key interconnected theological insights. These form a mosaic for Christian life, although Paul and the church often struggle and differ in their understanding of authentic existence in Christ.

God's Plan of Salvation

Central to Christian theology is an understanding of God's plan of salvation, that God now acts in and through Christ to bring all humanity to the fullness of life. Paul notes that "in Christ God was reconciling the world to himself" (2 Cor 5:19). "For since death came through a human being, the resurrection of the dead has also come through a human being; for as all die in Adam, so all will be made alive in Christ" (1 Cor 15:21-22). In the Corinthian letters, Paul proclaims the death and resurrection of Christ, according to the Scriptures, as the source of new life for those united to him. "Christ died for our sins in accordance with the scriptures, and that he was buried, and that he was raised on the third day in accordance with the scriptures..." (1 Cor 15:3-4). Paul's insight regarding the centrality and significance of the Christ-event has a functional dimension, that is, *Christ died for us*. In fact, all Paul's theological insights tend to have this functional emphasis. He is vitally interested in the significance of God's action in Christ, and that is the purpose of his theological reflection, not abstract conceptualization.

Believers As a New Creation in the Spirit

Because of this mystery of salvation, believers share in a new existence as a new creation filled with the Spirit of the Lord. "So if anyone is in Christ, there is a new creation: everything old has passed away; see, everything has become new!" (2 Cor 5:17). Paul engages the community to reflect on its identity as believers. Within the community are the gifts of the Spirit: "All these are activated by one and the same Spirit, who allots to each one individually just as the Spirit chooses" (1 Cor 12:11). This dynamic community grows and changes, for it is "always open to development and in touch with the practicalities of the moment" (Banks 15). Paul's insight regarding the intimate connection between Christ and Christians in his conversion leads him to describe the community as the body of Christ (1 Cor 12:12-13). Not only does an interrelationship exist among members of the body, but unity, equality, freedom, and diversity permeate Paul's reflections on church. Paul's understanding of church emanates from his understanding of Christ; ecclesiology flows from Christology.

Community Transformation in the Fullness of Time

The Corinthian community of believers experience so many of the transformational gifts of the Spirit that it believes that the fullness of time has come. This realized eschatology is at odds with Paul's understanding of the mystery of Christ. An atmosphere of expectation and hope permeates the apostle's understanding of the end times. For him the present is only a partial realization of what we will experience in the future: "...in a moment, in the twinkling of an eye, at the last trumpet. For the trumpet will sound, and the dead will be raised imperishable, and we will be changed. For this perishable body must put on imperishability, and this mortal body must put on immortality" (1 Cor 15:52-53). Apocalyptic thought and imagery, used and modified by Paul, so affects his thinking that some commentators see this as the coherent center of his theology (Beker, *Apostle*, 145.262). Paul changes his view of the end times between 1 and 2 Corinthians (1 Cor 7:29; 15:51), sensing that God's final victory is far ahead of us. However the tension continues in his letters between what we now experience and what is still ahead of us (2 Cor 4:4; 5:17). Likewise, Paul remains convinced that Christ's death and resurrection inaugurate the new age of salvation (Ridderbos 44). "'Fullness of time' is...the beginning of a new epoch, while the end of time is still to be expected" (Fiorenza, *Memory*, 186).

Paul's focus on eschatology stimulates hope and contributes to a different perspective on Christian life, suffering, and death, on-going challenges for the Corinthian church. For Paul this hope offers consolation in his ministry. "For this slight momentary affliction is preparing us for an eternal weight of glory beyond all measure, because we look not at what can be seen but at what cannot be seen; for what can be seen is temporary, but what cannot be seen is eternal" (2 Cor 4:17-18). However, the apostle knows that believers do experience the presence and power of the Lord in the community, and this realization affects his views of their potential for growth.

Believers' Unity in Christ

Since Christians abide in Christ they share a unity and equality that characterizes their relationships with one another. Furthermore, freedom is also theirs because of the transformational presence of the Lord. These theological insights affect the various issues Paul addresses in the Corinthian correspondence. His key insight regarding the death and resurrection of Christ has profound implications for the community, and he exhorts the community to live accordingly. The apostle's reflections on love and reconciliation emerge from his basic conviction of what God does for us through Christ.

Paul integrates his theological insights into his discussion of important issues in the Corinthian church and into his assessment of their difficult mutual relationship. As we recall these key points, we can identify the faith convictions that affect Paul's proclamation, ministry, and writing. Such theological reflection on God, the world, and Christian life sets in motion a dynamic that engages readers in the first, and twenty-first, century.

Understanding of God in the Corinthian Correspondence

Paul's Understanding of God in 1 and 2 Corinthians

As we read these letters, we can identify the early Christians' understanding of God in the descriptions Paul uses. While the Corinthian letters address the situation of church and could lead to an inadequate appreciation of the transcendent, we glimpse great diversity of expression as Paul reflects on his experience of God, Jesus, and the Spirit. Although the influence of patriarchy affects the language of Scripture, the reality of God goes far beyond the language any generation uses to describe God. What we can appreciate in these early Christian writings is the initial clarification of the relationship between the Father, Jesus, and the Spirit, and the numerous expressions that convey the Christian belief in one God. In addition, the ending of 2 Corinthians is unique, for in no other place does Paul bring together three names of God or offer such a comprehensive description of their effect on Christian life (Martin 114). "The grace of the Lord Jesus Christ, the love of God, and the communion of the Holy Spirit be with all of you" (2 Cor 13:13). Paul's understanding of God comes from his Jewish background and his vision of God's revelation in Jesus. Therefore, we can expect an intertwining of images and descriptions in the Corinthian letters as we explore Paul's testimony regarding God, Jesus, and Spirit.

Images of God

Paul's understanding of "one God, the Father, from whom are all things and for whom we exist" (1 Cor 8:6) would be typical of his religious environment as a Hellenistic Jew (1 Cor 1:3; 12:6; 15:24; 2 Cor 1:2-3; 5:18; 11:31). In addition to the father image, God is merciful (2 Cor 1:3; 4:1), faithful (1 Cor 1:9; 10:13; 2 Cor 1:18), the creator and source of life (1 Cor 1:30; 8:6; 2 Cor 6:16), powerful (1 Cor 2:5), judge (1 Cor 4:4; 11:32), knowing (1 Cor 3:20; 8:3; 2 Cor 5:11), and wise (1 Cor 1:21). Paul reflects on wisdom in this letter because of the Corinthian's different understanding of it. "But we speak God's wisdom, secret and hidden, which God decreed before the ages for our glory" (1 Cor 2:7). Paul does not proclaim the mystery of God in lofty words (1 Cor 2:1), but "these things God has revealed to us through the Spirit; for the Spirit searches everything, even the depths of God" (1 Cor 2:10).

From his understanding, Paul indicates that God gives growth (1 Cor 3:6), grace (1 Cor 3:10; 15:10; 2 Cor 8:1), peace (1 Cor 7:15; 14:33), a body (1 Cor 15:37), immortality (1 Cor 15:53; 2 Cor 1:9), and victory through Jesus Christ (1 Cor 15:57). God loves (2 Cor 9:7; 13:13), and "is able to provide you with every blessing in abundance, so that by always having enough of everything, you may share abundantly in every good work" (2 Cor 9:8). Indescribable gifts come from God (2 Cor 9:15), with reconciliation noted in light of community problems (2 Cor 5:18-19). Paul mentions the kingdom of God only eight times in his authentic letters and five of these occur in 1 Corinthians (4:20; 6:9.10; 15:24.50).

Paul understands God in new ways because of the profound revelation in Jesus. "For the message about the cross is foolishness to those who are perishing, but to us who are being saved it is the power of God" (1 Cor 1:18). Likewise, God calls us to belief (1 Cor 1:24), raises Jesus from the dead, will raise us (1 Cor 6:14; 15:15), and reveals glory in Jesus (2 Cor 4:6). God is "the God and Father of the Lord Jesus" (2 Cor 11:31), and we are sons and daughters (2 Cor 6:18). Paul reflects on God's displeasure with the ancestors (1 Cor 10:5), notes the subjection of all (1 Cor 15:27), and indicates that God appoints gifted persons in the church (1 Cor 12:28).

Many of these attributes and images of God resonate with the Jewish Scriptures, such as "Father," "creator," and "judge." But others, while reminiscent of the Jewish Scriptures, result from the revelation of Jesus as the power and wisdom of God. "The Pauline Christians believe in one God, sole creator of the universe and ultimate judge of all human actions. In most respects their monotheism is exactly that of Judaism....Yet they also accord to the crucified and resurrected Messiah, Jesus, some titles and functions that in the Bible and Jewish tradition were attributed only to God" (Meeks 190).

Portrayal of Jesus

The Corinthian correspondence contains many descriptions of Jesus, focusing primarily on his significance for us. Jesus is the Lord who sanctifies (1 Cor 1:2.9; 6:11; 2 Cor 1:19; 4:5; 8:9) and gives grace (1 Cor 1:3-4; 2 Cor 13:13). He is God's Son (1 Cor 1:9; 15:28; 2 Cor 1:19), the power and wisdom of God (1 Cor 1:24), the crucified Lord of glory (1 Cor 2:2.8; 5:7), who "died for our sins in accordance with the scriptures" (1 Cor 15:3; 2 Cor 5:4.15.21). Paul's own experience of Jesus as risen Lord leads him to refer to the power of the resurrection (1 Cor 5:4; 15:4.12.20; 2 Cor 12:9). Christ becomes "for us wisdom from God, and righteousness and sanctification and redemption" (1 Cor 1:30; 6:11), and we are one with him (1 Cor 6:15). Although Christ is the new/last Adam and the life-giving spirit (1 Cor 15:20-28.45) who is from heaven (1 Cor 15:47), he is also subject to God (1 Cor 15:28).

Paul's understanding of Jesus brings together various components of his religious background. In these letters, the apostle associates Jesus with wisdom, and "his ideas of Christ's pre-existence and mediatorship in creation are a result of his transferring the characteristics of the divine Wisdom to Christ" (Kim 117). The sending of the Son, in light of Paul's understanding of the prophets who were also sent (Isa 6:8; Jer 1:7; Ezek 2:3), "underlines the Son's commissioning, obedience, and special relationship to God" (Ziesler 40-41). Paul's understanding of Christ is far simpler than later theology, but he is convinced that God acts in and through Christ on our behalf (2 Cor 3:4). He also sees Christ as the image of God (2 Cor 4:4), worthy of imitation (1 Cor 11:1), above us as head (1 Cor 11:3), and with us as one Lord (1 Cor 6:11; 8:6). Paul also reflects on the community as members of Christ's body, and he draws out the significance of this reality in his preaching (1 Cor 3:11; 12:27). Interestingly, in these letters, Paul uses the titles Christ, Christ Jesus, or Jesus Christ, rather than the personal name, Jesus, indicating the Lord's significance in the salvation of humankind. Paul centers his faith on God's action in Christ. Furthermore, what Paul says of Christ does not take way from his affirmation of the oneness of God: "yet for us there is one God, the Father, from whom are all things and for whom we exist, and one Lord, Jesus Christ, through whom are all things and through whom we exist" (1 Cor 8:6).

The dual perspective of cross (1 Cor 1:18-25) and resurrection (1 Cor 15:1-58) stemming from his own conversion experience shapes Paul's understanding of Jesus. In the early Christian movement, Paul and his associates recognized the generative potential of this powerful symbol. "The node around which Pauline beliefs crystallized was the crucifixion and resurrection of God's son, the Messiah" (Meeks 180). Paul links together death and resurrection, drawing out implications for Christian life (1 Cor 15:15; 2 Cor 4:10-11). However, the apostle also understands God's ultimate victory as future in the final resurrection of the dead (Beker, *Apostle*, 180).

Furthermore, Paul has little interest in "the past event of Jesus' crucifixion, but in the recurring event of the word of the cross" (Wire 49) (1 Cor 1:17-2:16). This word speaks about God, power, and weakness, for the "cross is the place where *God* meets humanity, saving them, or sentencing them in case they do not acknowledge God's presence at this place of contempt" (Lampe 119-120). Paul expresses this conviction in his summary of an early creedal formula. "For the love of Christ urges us on, because we are convinced that one has died for all; therefore all have died" (2 Cor 5:14). So many of Paul's reflections seem to be linked to this central mystery of faith! He pursues its meaning even though the Corinthian church sees his preaching of the cross as folly.

Witness to the resurrection is also integral to Paul's preaching. "If Christ has not been raised, your faith is futile and you are still in your sins. Then those also who have died in Christ have perished" (1 Cor 15:18). Christians share in the fruits of the resurrection, for it is not only a past event but results in the abiding presence of the Lord (Swain 116). Union between Christ and Christians, an insight so central to Paul's theology, culminates hope of future of glory. In addition, Christ's resurrection begins the process of transformation—a new age dawns! Paul connects various elements of faith, such as the resurrection of Christ and Christians, future fullness of life, and present transformation, in a way that challenges the church's thinking. "Examine yourselves to see whether you are living in the faith. Test yourselves. Do you not realize that Jesus Christ is in you?" (2 Cor 13:5). If Christians are "in Christ, there is a new creation: everything old has passed away; see, everything has become new! (2 Cor 5:17).

Witness to the Spirit

1 and 2 Corinthians offer testimony to the Spirit, its presence and power in the faith community. The Spirit of God reveals, teaches, gives understanding, and offers gifts to us (1 Cor 2:10-14; 12:4). This Spirit dwells within us (1 Cor 3:16; 6:19), sanctifies, and justifies (1 Cor 6:11). As believers we all share the one Spirit, a conviction that Paul will use in his understanding of church (H. Doohan, *Vision*, 149-165). "Now there are varieties of gifts, but the same Spirit" (1 Cor 12:4) that contribute to the building up of the body of Christ. In this faith community, the Spirit also creates a new set of relationships: "For in the one Spirit we were all baptized into one body—Jews or Greeks, slaves or free—and we were all made to drink of one Spirit" (1 Cor 12:13). This Spirit of the living God gives life (1 Cor 3:3.6), is associated with ministry (1 Cor 3:8), creates unity (2 Cor 13:13), and is the guarantee of eternal life (2 Cor 5:5).

The Spirit is also the Spirit of Christ, "for this comes from the Lord, the Spirit" (2 Cor 3:18), who is the crucified Lord of glory (1 Cor 2:8). "Indeed it is crucial for Paul that Spirit-experience be Christ-experience....Christ and the Spirit in effect define one another" (Ziesler 46; cf Ridderbos 88). In grounding his understanding of the Spirit in Christ, Paul associates the Spirit with the person and work of Jesus, the crucifixion, and the risen Lord.

The apostle also identifies the implications of the presence of the Spirit *for us*, an interest in all his theological reflection. "Now the Lord is the Spirit, and where the Spirit of the Lord is, there is freedom" (2 Cor 3:17). This Spirit is a transforming power in Christian life (2 Cor 5:17; 1 Cor 2:12-20; 12 and 14) and offers us a new way of experiencing reality, for "the

Spirit gives life" (2 Cor 3:6). In this respect, the Spirit is the authentic sign of the new age, begun but not yet fully realized (Martin 127). The Corinthian church, enthralled as it was by the extraordinary gifts of the Spirit, felt they experienced the full realization of Spirit's presence. However, Paul identifies many aspects of the Spirit's presence in order to expand their focus and challenge their views of the end times.

"The Spirit counted as authority par excellence in the Pauline communities" (Meeks 138). When the apostle cannot not draw on tradition to validate his point, he calls on the Spirit: "I think that I too have the Spirit of God" (1 Cor 7:40). This Spirit unifies members of the community and fosters their sense of mutual responsibility. "To each is given the manifestation of the Spirit for the common good" (1 Cor 12:7). The energy of the Spirit, so evident as we read the Corinthian letters, gives us a real sense of God's new creation in Christ. In Paul's understanding, the Spirit is God's presence and power at work in the world and in the church. We all share in this one Spirit by our union with the Lord in faith, and the Spirit fills us, the community of believers, with a variety of gifts.

The images of God in the Corinthian letters form a basis for later theological developments, such as the doctrine of the Trinity. However, in the Pauline communities, we have only the seeds of this later synthesis. The apostle, Paul, simply communicates his understanding of God, revealed to him in Christ and the Christian community, and experienced in the presence of the Spirit. As we reflect on Paul's gospel and theology, we can identify remarkable implications for our Christian life and ministry.

Challenges to Faith and Implications for Christian Life

The letters to the Corinthians reveal the Gospel Paul preaches, the tradition he receives, the theological insights he develops, the understanding of God, Jesus, and the Spirit he shares. For the church in Corinth, and for ourselves as well, Paul's letters offer challenges to our faith and force us to rethink aspects of our Christian life in terms of that faith.

Paul's understanding of the Gospel comes to him, most vividly, in his conversion experience. While Paul tells us nothing of the details of that religious encounter itself, he does identify its impact on his life. He now understands Jesus differently, has a mission to preach the Gospel to the Gentiles, and views all reality in terms of God's salvific action in Christ. Paul is convinced of the power of the Gospel to transform existence. He preaches out of a personal experience of the Lord, and whether or not the community agrees with his perspective, they know his commitment. In liturgical ministry we proclaim the Gospel, we speak of faith realities, we understand our mission to mediate, proclaim, and celebrate. Do we preach the good news from our own experience of the Lord Jesus? Are we willing to change in our understanding of God's action in the world as Paul did? Do we cling to religious experience for its own sake, or do we focus on our call to serve? Do we allow God to work, or are we too concerned about our own impact on others?

Paul received the Gospel in God's revelation to him, but also from those who were Christians before him. While respecting the tradition, Paul assumes leadership in its adaptation and interpretation for a Gentile audience. To do this faithfully, he had to identify the essential components of the message, as well as reflect on the experiences of the community. In our preaching of the word, do we respect the tradition handed on to us? Do we make the Gospel real for our hearers by interpreting it for our community and world? Can we identify the essence of faith and let go of the non-essentials? Paul could grow and change in his understanding as an apostle. How have we grown in our understanding of our faith?

The letters convey some of Paul's theological insights and their significance. He understands the meaning of Christ's death and resurrection for his own life and ministry. He senses the possibilities of Christian life because of his understanding of the Spirit of the risen Lord. Within the letters, his theological reflection develops and deepens as he responds to changing circumstances in the community's life. Paul's attitude seems to be one of discovery as he integrates his own early background with the new faith he has received. Does our reflection on God, the world, and ourselves take into consideration our background, early experiences, and maturity in faith? How open are we to new theological reflection in a changing world? How does our understanding of Christ's death and resurrection affect our views of suffering, ministry, and Christian life?

Paul was not a speculative theologian, an ivory tower professor, or an aloof preacher, but a servant of the community immersed in the concrete realities of Christian life. In fact, some would say that his "theologizing is more important for us than his theology because his theologizing takes place as a form of social relations" (Peterson 30). Does not this describe what we do as we struggle to understand the faith we have received? As pastors and ministers, how does our community become the forum and the sphere of our theological reflection? As pastoral theologians, do we call the community to celebrate its life, with its problems and promise, in our worship together?

Within these letters, Paul describes his understanding of God in a variety of ways. He imagines what God is like from his experience of the risen Lord and of the Spirit's presence. He is an original thinker in the way he connects ideas and images, and his belief in one God does not change with his conversion. Rather, Paul sees God differently and, perhaps, more completely because of Jesus. How has your experience of God changed in your adult life? What image would you use to convey your understanding of God's action in your life? Who is Jesus for you? How does the presence and power of the Spirit affect who you are and what you do?

Reflecting on Paul's understanding of the Gospel is an exciting and revitalizing experience because we become engaged in what was, for him, a dynamic process, rather than a static repetition of ideas. With an understanding of the content of the Gospel and the theological development of the early church, we can now examine various issues in the Corinthian church and attempt to understand the principles at stake when Paul challenges the community in terms of its Christian life.

For Personal and Group Reflection

1. The Gospel was proclaimed by word of mouth long before communities had access

to the written word. What is the good news that we preach as ministers of the Word? What is its relationship to the written Scriptures?

2. Paul appreciated and handed on the tradition in the early church. Which aspects of the Christian tradition do you find particularly significant in your life and ministry?

3. Paul not only handed on the tradition, but he adapted and interpreted it in light of community needs. How do we as church adapt the Gospel message to new times and situations?

4. Paul understood the essence of Gospel in God's action in the death and resurrection of Jesus. What are the essentials of Christian faith? What can be changed in the living out of our faith?

5. Paul wove theological insight into his discussion of issues and concerns in the Corinthian correspondence. How can a ministry team reflect theologically on the issues and concerns facing the parish community or Christian group?

6. Paul described God as Father, Son, and Spirit. Using words and images, describe your experience and understanding of God.

7. Paul's faith understanding of Christ initially came from his conversion experience. Who is Jesus for you? How does Paul's understanding of the Lord challenge your own views?

8. The Spirit is the sign of Christ's presence and power in the community. How do you see the Spirit at work in the community to which you belong?

9. How does your understanding of God affect the way you live and minister?

10. Paul's understanding of the Gospel and its implications transformed his life and that of the early church. What difference does your faith make in the way you live, work, and minister?

Chapter Four

The Corinthian Church's Life and Value Systems

Paul's preaching of the Gospel led to the establishment of faith communities that witnessed to their belief in their daily lives. Although he greets many individuals in his letters, his apostolic focus was on the founding of churches. His conversion of households, with their special environment and diverse membership, contributed to the development of the church and to the continuance of missionary endeavors. We could say that Paul's interest was in the creation of community, a community called church or *ecclesia*, that we come to know quite well through the Corinthian correspondence.

Since the publication of "The Significance of the Early House Churches" by Floyd Filson in 1939, the impact of house churches on the development of the early church has been examined extensively. These Christian households created a setting where faith grew, values were clarified, and responsibility for the spread of the Gospel was assumed according to the gifts of the Spirit. Our earliest insight into Christian life comes from New Testament testimony to these local churches in the letters of Paul. The vibrancy of the interaction and the attractiveness of the experience within and among these house churches make us wonder at the level of faith their members must have possessed.

Paul leaves us with many descriptions of these ecclesial communities in his letters to the Corinthians. Underlying his use of the "body of Christ," "temple," and "new creation" is a call for unity, equality, freedom, and mutual love. These values provide the tools by which Paul and the community assess the gifts of the Spirit and discern the directions of community growth. They struggle together to identify the practical consequences of living the Gospel in a Gentile environment. The community of believers understand their call in Christ and their union with him and one another. In 1 and 2 Corinthians, Paul builds on this understanding in order to affirm the community's faith, challenge its direction, or respond to its questions.

These letters also demonstrate how Paul deals with issues and questions in the early church. The Corinthian's concerns emerge in these letters, such as proper use of freedom in eating food offered to idols, women's options in marriage, and celibate commitments. Whether the questions are ethical concerns, roles in the community, spiritual gifts, or the collection for the poor, Paul and the community wrestle with the issues and attempt to discern the Gospel challenge. At the same time, they witness to the growth taking place in the early church as members clarify its direction through dialogue and debate.

As we explore the values and life of the early church in this chapter, we notice that some of the insights and response to issues are timeless. However, we also see first century cultural and political influences at work in our biblical text. As liturgical leaders and educators, we have the task of identifying the perennial values, appreciating the origin of our traditions, and reinterpreting the message for our contemporary households of faith. Paul's interest was always on the impact of decisions on community life. This focus is important since it is our shared life as church that we celebrate in worship.

Households of Faith and the Local Church

The Role of the House Churches

The Corinthian correspondence, written in the decade of the 50s, offers us a very early insight into the development of the Christian community. The first written New Testament references we have to house churches come from Paul, and these offer a glimpse into their development, purpose, and membership, particularly in the letters to the Corinthians. Issues regarding leadership, social customs, and communal celebrations quickly surface as the community, in this setting, seeks to understand the implications of the Gospel message. While we know something of the eventual growth of these households of faith from later New Testament and early church writings, the freshness of the Corinthian dialogue allows us to sense the importance of this early component in our Christian understanding of church.

Witness to Existence of House Churches

While the Corinthian church has little or no formal leadership, the beginnings of organization emerge in the households such as that of Stephanas, mentioned only in Corinthians (Barrett, *1 Corinthians*, 24). "Now, brothers and sisters, you know that members of the household of Stephanas were the first converts in Achaia, and they have devoted themselves to the service of the saints" (1 Cor 16:15). Paul recognizes the ministry of this house church, and we know from the letters that others exist in Corinth and elsewhere. The early reference to Chloe's people not only refers to a household of faith but attests that women provide leadership in such households (1 Cor 1:11; Philem 1-2; Col 4:15; Acts 16:15) (Fiorenza, *Memory*, 246). Writers often name and associate Prisca and Aquila with their house church in Rome and later in Ephesus (1 Cor 16:19; Rom 16:3.5; Acts 18:2; 2 Tim 4:19). In addition to Stephanas (1 Cor 1:16), Gaius (1 Cor 1:14; Rom 16:23) and Crispus (1 Cor 1:14; Acts 18:8) are heads of households in Corinth. Greetings at the end of the letter to the Romans, written from Corinth, attest to prominent people in the local church and begin to fill out the picture of leadership roles in the community.

Luke in Acts of Apostles also confirms the existence of households of faith in the earliest period of church life. While Paul speaks of the conversion of a household once (1 Cor 1:16), "The Acts makes such a household conversion almost a theme in itself (Acts 10:2; 16:15; 18:8; cf Jn 4:53)" (Branick 18). Luke offers a number of summary descriptions of these gatherings of the early church, identifying the components of their life (Acts 2:46; 5:42). Furthermore, "The Christian home appears here in exact counterpoint to the Jewish Temple" (Branick 14). Homes of well-to-do citizens provided space for preaching, worship, eucharistic sharing, and social interaction (Fiorenza, *Memory*, 175). This household setting provides the context for understanding the family imagery and language in the scriptures.

Did these house churches originate with Paul and the Christian community? Or were homes used for religious as well as social purposes in other settings? We know of house-based synagogues (Crosby 35; Meyers 31) and home-based communities similar to the Christian house churches from writings and excavations. The household in the Jewish community was "the primary place for the transmission of the faith," for prayer, and for mealtime blessings. On special feasts such as Passover, Philo suggests that each house takes on "the character of the holiness of the Temple" (Branick 45-46). Religious rituals were also part of Hellenistic households where many homes had private worship shrines with wives assisting their husbands at the family altar (Love 23; Branick 44). Interestingly, the octagonal church of St. Peter in Capernaum may be built over excavations of a Jewish-Christian house church dating to the third century CE. However, some believe that the first-century edifice below that house may be the actual residence of Peter (Meyers 29). Homes were important gathering places in the biblical period and various missionaries utilized these places for the extension of their mission.

In addition, the home was the basic economic and political unit of society. Paul uses the words *oikos* and *oikia*, meaning "economy" and "economics" to describe the household with its persons and property (Branick 36). The concept is much broader than our understanding of family or extended family. The diversity and richness of this setting allowed for a variety of forms of celebration, sharing, prayer, and worship. Women had a definite role within the households of faith because the Gospel preached by Paul challenged the traditional relationships within religion and society (Gal 3:28) (Fiorenza, *Memory*, 176).

Paul's Use of Households of Faith

Paul utilized the households for a variety of purposes, such as a base for his missionary work, an assembly place for the celebration of the Lord's Supper, prayer, and preaching, and a locus for Christian fellowship. This gathering, while localized, expanded its horizons and influence by networking with other households in a city, forming a local church. Hospitality was a core value and the interpersonal relationships provided an atmosphere that could foster the faith that brought them together. The house church was "the training ground for the Christian leaders" who were to continue the mission after the loss of "apostolic" leaders (Filson 112).

The Christians community developed a sense of belonging, a social identity, and rituals for celebration. The house church became a sacred context for redefining social worlds, and the Corinthian church would struggle with its social and economic diversity. Dealing with social stratification within a faith community differed significantly from the lived reality in Corinth.

Membership, Setting, and Lifestyle

What did the community look like in terms of membership? What were the households like in size and structure? Life in the crowded city of Corinth lacked private spaces for the ordinary and poor citizen. Property was a sign of wealth, and the large homes of the early Christians became the gathering places for the community. The heads of these households would possess high social status, and they would welcome all members of the church into their dwelling. The commingling of rich and poor, slave and free, men and women was a stark contrast to the typical experience in the patriarchal households of the time (1 Cor 1:26; 12:13).

Hosting the local gathering or the city-wide assemblies was the privilege of those who owned homes large enough for the gathering.

A typical urban extended family under one roof would be about fifty people connected by bonds of kinship and friendship (Love 22). When the church assembled in these homes, the group included close friends of the host who reclined at their places in the triclinium, and the rest sat at inferior places in the atrium (Murphy-O'Connor, *Corinth*, 158-159). The triclinium would hold about twenty persons if you removed all the couches (Branick 39-42). The maximum number in the atrium was fifty, but the true number was between thirty and forty if you account for decorative urns and art work (Murphy-O'Connor, *Corinth*, 156). Thus, when the local church met, the numbers would range between thirty and forty people who represented different social backgrounds. These differences between the groups led to the problems Paul addresses in 1 Corinthians 11.

The diagrams on the following pages indicate the floor plan and space utilization in villas that were comparable to house churches in the biblical period.

The Corinthian Church's Life and Value Systems

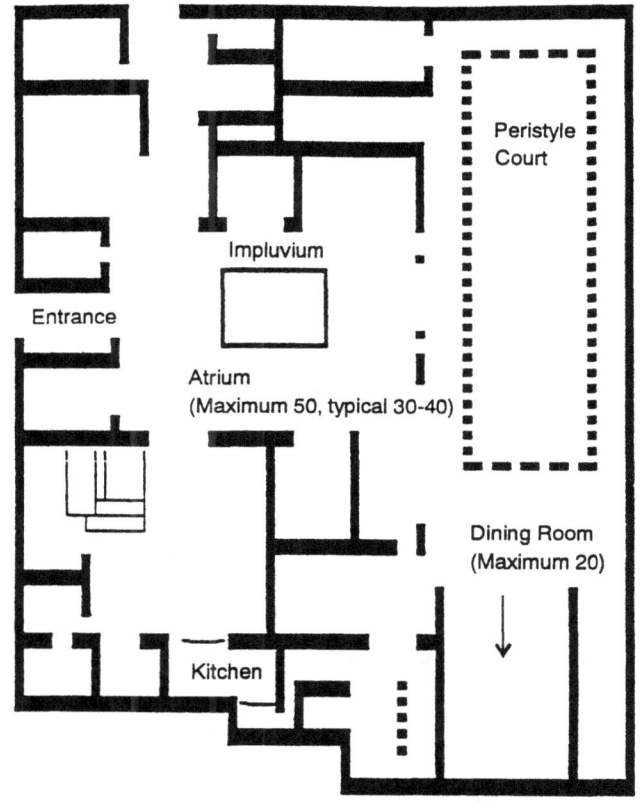

TYPICAL LAYOUT OF A HOUSEHOLD USED AS A CHURCH:
HOUSE OF THE VETTI AT POMPEII

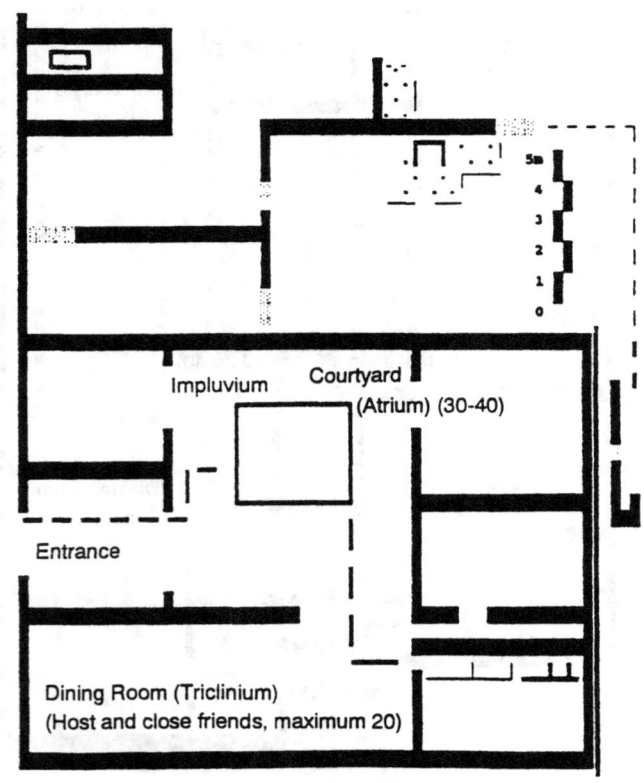

TYPICAL LAYOUT OF A HOUSEHOLD USED AS A CHURCH:
THE ROMAN VILLA AT ANAPLOGA

Following Vatican II home gatherings and liturgical celebrations occurred fairly regularly in our own communities. These small groups were certainly reminiscent of the early church and even today provide an experience of intimacy for the community. Christian households of faith were associations of equals, unlike the Jewish households of the time which were patriarchal in structure, although they allowed women greater freedom than their Greek counterparts (Fiorenza, *Memory*, 181; Verner 44-45). Within the traditional Greek and Roman household, prestige and privilege ranked high, and the households were typically headed by men (Verner 79). Given this background, the Christian experience of a discipleship of equals became a counter-cultural witness. Faith convictions removed the barriers and led to an association of equals within these Christian households. Since Christians could still be members of other households, tensions would arise as they moved between these different settings. Reordering relationships within the community of faith that were in direct contrast to society's norms was a tremendous challenge for Paul and the church in Corinth, a challenge that still affects many Christian communities throughout the world to this day.

Interestingly, Paul focuses primarily on relationships within the house churches and seems to neglect the broader political and social ramifications of equality in Christ. He does not challenge societal structures of slavery and submission of women. However, for contemporary Christians, an awareness that our beginnings as church took place in home gatherings, as well as synagogue and Temple, can help us identify the spirit of the gathering and the deep sense of personal commitment in the early church. We can also reflect on the values formed in church gatherings today, and how these impact the society in which we live.

The collegial structure of these early house churches soon gave way to strong authority structures and restrictive household codes (Col 3:18-4:1; Eph 5:21-6:9; 1 Tim 2:1-6:2) (Jeffers 122; Fiorenza, *Memory*, 286-287). Around 150 CE private residences were adapted and dedicated for the exclusive use of the church, and in 314 CE the first basilicas appeared (Branick 15, 129). "The Christians meeting in dedicated churches and basilicas show an understanding of themselves different from that of the Christians meeting in the house churches. Leadership became concentrated in fewer hands, the hands of a special class of holy people. Church activities became stylized ritual. The building rather than the community became the temple of God" (Branick 15). However, these later changes are a contrast to the experience of the Corinthian church.

The Understanding of Church in the Letters to the Corinthians

The Local Church

The households in Corinth were the gathering places of the church, and local households assembled together as "the whole church" in an area, as 1 Corinthians 14:23 may indicate. Paul also speaks of aggregates of churches or congregations in different areas in his correspondence (1 Cor 4:17; 7:17; 11:16; 16:1). Precedent for the *ekklesia* or church may be found not only in the households, but also in voluntary associations, the synagogue, and the philosophic or rhetorical schools found in cities such as Corinth (Meeks 75-84). However, in biblical usage, the idea of gathering and assembling is integral to the early understanding of church (Banks 41). "According to Paul it is the *ekklesia*, the 'assembly of the saints' who have equal access to God in the Spirit and are therefore coequal members in the body of Christ. Social roles in this *ekklesia* are not based on natural or social differences but on charismatic giftedness" (Fiorenza, *Bread*, 75).

Paul's understanding of church takes the Christian *ekklesia* beyond other groups that may have offered precedents, since this group shares a faith relationship to the Lord and each other that empowers the community membership. This "church of God that is in Corinth" is a community of believers that exhibits the power of God in action (2 Cor 1:1-11). Because of this dimension the church is a sacrament or sign of a new reality, a new creation (2 Cor 5:17).

While Paul uses many metaphors for church, such as building, temple, field, and body, all have a dynamic rather than static quality to them (1 Cor 3:5-11.16; 6:19; 12:12; 2 Cor 6:16). "So with yourselves; since you are eager for spiritual gifts, strive to excel in them for building up the church" (1 Cor 14:12). Paul utilizes the idea of upbuilding of the church in many contexts in his letters, challenging the Corinthian church in its mutual responsibility (Ridderbos 429). The idea of an assembly, empowered by the Spirit of God for the purpose of building itself up in faith, is an understanding of church that remains appropriate for our own celebrations and worship. In fact, the models of church that emerge in Paul's letters, the people of God, the new creation, the new humanity or mystical (one new) person, and the body of Christ, challenge us to become what we are called to be in Christ (H. Doohan, *Vision*, 144-165). These models have the power to energize the early church as well as embody its reality. These and other models can do the same for us today.

The Community As the Body of Christ

Of the many descriptions that the apostle uses in his letters, understanding the community as the body of Christ is a typically Pauline formulation. "The theme of the Body first appears in 1 Cor, and the way in which Paul formulates his remarks clearly indicates that it formed part of his oral preaching in Corinth" (Murphy-O'Connor, *Corinth*, 165). In this image of a living organism, Paul conveys the reality of life shared in union with Christ through the one Spirit. This unique theological vision allows the local community to use this understanding of itself to critique its life, growth, and decisions. The dynamism inherent in the image of body creates a tension between unity and diversity, while affirming both dimensions. The Corinthian community must learn to discern directions within these very broad parameters that call for mutual respect and trust. Paul, while strong in the expression of his views in his correspondence, does not suggest uniformity or blending differences within the church. Because of his insight into the implications of being the body of Christ, we can continue to appreciate the historical, cultural, and ethnic diversity within the Christian churches today, as well as the tremendously diverse religious expressions in our world.

As we reflect on our identity as an ecclesial community, we can appreciate the solidarity that is ours as members of the body of Christ, as well as our interdependence. Mutuality in love and responsibility becomes the living challenge for Christians as we explore the implications of our participation in Christ. For the Corinthians, as for ourselves, this understanding of church translates into the values and principles they embody in their lives and use in their decisions.

Values and Principles for Interaction within the Church

When we read sections such as chapters 5-12 in 1 Corinthians, we become aware that Paul does not simply answer questions raised by the community, but he operates out of principles that will enable the community to deal with other issues that need discernment. These principles emerge from Paul's convictions regarding Christian transformation in Christ and his understanding of church.

Paul encourages the community to grow in its ability to make judgments. "Brothers and sisters, do not be children in your thinking; rather, be infants in evil, but in thinking be adults" (1 Cor 14:20). He sets parameters for living the Gospel but involves himself in the community and becomes a model for them. His view of Christian life includes a rigorous involvement of mind and heart that will often set the Corinthians and Paul on different tracks and lead them to conflicting solutions (Sampley 117-118). Mutual responsibility seems to underlie so many of his exhortations, as we will see. Values of unity, Christian love, freedom, and equality frame Paul's discussion of issues and enable him to identify the use of gifts in the community of faith. Family settings for church gatherings provide the atmosphere for conversations and create the conditions for exchange.

Unity in the Church

The principle of unity is foundational to Paul's understanding of the Corinthian church and to relationships between Jerusalem and the Gentile churches (1 Cor 12:2-31;

10:14-22; 6:13-20). "The real and supporting ground of the whole conception of the people of God as the body of Christ, however, lies in the unity of the church with Christ himself. This unity is...not merely in the first place of a spiritual kind, but goes beyond that" (Ridderbos 394). The starting point for unity in the Christian community is our relationship in and with Christ. From this reality flows our communion with one another. Paul understands that Christian baptism brings about this unity when he states: "For in the one Spirit we were all baptized into one body—Jews or Greeks, slaves or free—and we were all made to drink of one Spirit" (1 Cor 12:13). The Corinthian community celebrates this unity in its life and worship, and it struggles with its diversity, exercise of freedom, and mutual responsibility on a day to day basis. The practical applications of lofty principles, so appealing in these letters, offer guidelines for contemporary readers if we understand the inherent process and struggles suggested by the text.

Unity affects the fabric of our communal relationships. "If one member suffers, all suffer together with it; if one member is honored, all rejoice together with it" (1 Cor 12:26). It also shapes Paul's appeal regarding factions in the community. "Now I appeal to you, brothers and sisters, by the name of our Lord Jesus Christ, that all of you be in agreement and that there be no divisions among you, but that you be united in the same mind and the same purpose" (1 Cor 1:10). Paul focuses on relationships within the faith community because he understands that God communicates "not primarily through the written word and tradition, or mystical experience and cultic activity, but *through one another*" (Banks 111). This distinctive emphasis of Paul enables us to identify a starting point for our worship celebrations—the quality of our relationships (1 Cor 10:17). Paul will utilize this value as he deals with factions, social distinctions, the celebration of the Lord's Supper, and spiritual gifts. However, Paul also emphasizes the value of diversity, since the body of Christ cannot simply tolerate difference but actually depends on it! (1 Cor 12:22-24).

Christian Love

Paul speaks eloquently to the Corinthian church about Christian love in what probably is the most familiar chapter in this correspondence (1 Cor 13). Practical descriptions that resonate with family and community experience concretize Paul's understanding of Christian love. Perhaps the Corinthians were the opposite of what Paul suggests in 1 Corinthians 13:4-7; he may consider them to be impatient, unkind, jealous, boastful, resentful and so forth (Hurd 112). Whatever the reality, love is the essence of Christianity, and it has practical implications for our daily lives and all our relationships. "Let all that you do be done in love" (1 Cor 16:14).

The apostle to the Gentiles identifies many manifestations and requirements of love. For Paul, the church must stress "even more strongly the importance of respect for one another's convictions. The church is a place where people can afford to live together with different views, but that requires love" (Stendahl 61). In fact, the community experiences tension between love and freedom as it deals with issues such as food to idols (1 Cor 8-10). However, the Corinthians, like ourselves, understand that "the love of Christ urges us on" (2 Cor 5:14). This qualitatively different love relies on our union with the Lord for its strength and perseverance, not simply on good human values or qualities.

Freedom in the Spirit of Christ

Because of their baptism, members of the Christian community share freedom in Christ. "Now the Lord is the Spirit, and where the Spirit of the Lord is, there is freedom" (2 Cor 3:17). With this freedom comes responsibility toward others in all matters, even those of conscience (1 Cor 6:12; 8:9). Christian freedom is not so much an individual thing as it is a freedom that operates in believers in all circumstances (Murphy-O'Connor, "Eucharist," 382). Paul also sees the freedom of the individual as subordinate to the unity of the community (Gager 36). However, living out this understanding of freedom causes some difficulties in Corinth, particularly in women's roles, life choices for women and slaves (1 Cor 7; 14:33-36), and other issues (Wire 13). Paul claims freedom for himself as an apostle, but he also accepts restrictions to his own freedom (1 Cor 9:1-3). He says to this church: "For though I am free with respect to all, I have made myself a slave to all, so that I might win more of them" (1 Cor 9:19).

While the cornerstone of Paul's gospel is freedom, such freedom in Christ implies the price of sacrifice and suffering. The message to any community is that freedom, love, unity, and responsibility are all of a piece, and our discernment of choices requires sensitivity, prayer, and mutual respect. As we gather our communities together, we must create a religious climate in which we can discern appropriate directions for living out Gospel values.

Equality in Christ

Paul pursued a vision that transcended social norms and order, a vision reflected in baptismal confessions (1 Cor 12:13; Gal 3:28; Col 3:10-11). The closing claim in the formulas that "all are one in Christ" aligns equality with freedom for believers. An examination of the Corinthian issues demonstrates that this rhetoric of equality certainly appealed to women, but it also made more demands on women in some of their sexual roles, behavior in the Christian assembly, and use of spiritual gifts (Wire 82-83; Fiorenza, *Memory*, 236).

The focus of Paul's interest in the implications of the principle of equality is the community of faith. He leaves to others the expansion of this insight to include ever widening circles and society itself. The Corinthian correspondence rarely touches on the social and political dimensions of equality. What Paul does claim is equality in Christ in the faith community, while also recognizing the national, social, and sexual differences in place. "This creates genuine diversity within the community" (Banks 130).

The principle of equality is a difficult one to implement in some of our church structures and ecclesial ministries today. While Paul struggles with its consequences for women in Corinth, his writings do not justify the submission or silence of women. Wrestling with the language, context, and meaning of these difficult passages is our task in subsequent chapters. As preachers of the Word and religious educators of the community, we share a responsibility to understand and interpret the Gospel message, even when it becomes a prophetic challenge for our church.

The Presence of the Spirit's Gifts

Paul's understanding and experience of church convinces him of the presence of the gifts of the Spirit in all believers. "Now there are varieties of gifts, but the same Spirit; and there are varieties of services, but the same Lord; and there are varieties of activities, but it is the same God who activates all of them in everyone" (1 Cor 12:4-6). Christians share in these gifts of others while possessing different ones themselves, but all receive them from the same Spirit. These gifts are concrete manifestations of the power of God at work in the community. In the New Testament, the term *charism* occurs seventeen times, fourteen of them in Paul's writings, and eight in the Corinthian correspondence (1 Cor 1:7; 7:7; 12:4.9.28.30.31; 2 Cor 1:11) (Nardoni 69). In addition, Paul juxtaposes four terms in his letters: spiritual gifts/*pneumatika* (1 Cor 12:1); gifts of grace/*charismata* (1 Cor 12:4); services/*diakoniai* (1 Cor 12:5); workings/*energemata* (1 Cor 12:6a) (Hahn 239). All of these are particular manifestations of the fullness of grace given by Christ to the church (Ridderbos 448). "For in the one Spirit we were all baptized into one body—Jews or Greeks, slaves or free—and we were all made to drink of one Spirit" (1 Cor 12:13).

In 1 Corinthians, Paul offers a context for understanding the gifts and prioritizes them as well. The following table identifies the two Corinthian lists with the priorities Paul notes.

TABLE 7: THE GIFTS OF THE SPIRIT IN 1 CORINTHIANS

1 CORINTHIANS 12:8-12	1 CORINTHIANS 12:28-30
utterance of wisdom	first, apostles
utterance of knowledge	second, prophets
faith	third, teachers
gifts of healing	then, deeds of power
working of miracles	gifts of healing
prophecy	forms of assistance
discernment of spirits	forms of leadership
various kinds of tongues	various kinds of tongues
interpretation of tongues	interpretation

Elsewhere the apostle speaks of the gift of a particular lifestyle (1 Cor 7:7), the abundant spiritual gifts in the community (1 Cor 7-8), and the relationship of these gifts to Christian love (1 Cor 12:31). The proper use of the gifts includes building up the church (1 Cor 14:26), while recognizing its unity and transformation. Likewise, Christians cannot separate these charisms from their source or their function within the body of Christ. "The primary application of the body metaphor to the exercise of gifts is also clear. It is precisely through the *variety* of the various members' contributions that the unity of the community becomes manifest (12:6a), as well as in their proportionate strength (12:6b)" (Banks 65). Paul, as a leader, often identifies special gifts and facilitates their use within the community so that the Corinthians will grow as church. Each time our communities come together, the variety of gifts becomes evident. However, use of these gifts of the Spirit for the benefit of all is the ministerial challenge we all face as leaders in the church.

The gifts that we identify in these letters encompass every aspect of the church's life. Some of the gifts focus on the growth of understanding in the community, such as prophecy, teaching, and discernment; another group of pastoral gifts emphasizes the integrity and harmony of the community. The physical welfare of the community needs gifts of healing and financial assistance, while the unconscious life of the community grows with the gifts of prayer, tongues, and other manifestations of the Spirit (Banks 103). Can we identify within our faith communities, gifts that develop these four areas of life? In addition, do we understand and appreciate the gifts we have as Paul did (1 Cor 7:7; 15:10)?

The marvelous diversity of gifts is a value for Paul as he asks: "Are all apostles? Are all prophets? Are all teachers? Do all work miracles? Do all possess gifts of healing? Do all speak in tongues? Do all interpret? (1 Cor 12:29-30). To recognize and affirm the manifestations of the Spirit in another is the mark of a mature person. To assume responsibility for the gifts we have received and to use them generously on behalf of others takes a sustained commitment to Lord, even in times of misunderstanding and difficulties (2 Cor 4:8-12). Pastoral sensitivity to the effect of charisms on the community and its relationships is a challenge Paul faces, particularly in regard to speaking in tongues, a highly valued gift in Corinth, and to customs surrounding the women prophets in the church. We will examine Paul's handling of these issues in the next section. However, we might reflect on some of the extraordinary charisms in our own communities, workplaces, and families. How do we creatively utilize gifts of administration, prophetic challenge, non-traditional forms of healing, various cultural manifestations of spiritual values, or lifestyles different from our own? Paul seems to have an inclusive view of the gifts of the Spirit, and in this challenges us to broaden our perspective.

Corinthian Issues and Their Impact on Ecclesial Life

Paul utilizes principles and values such as the ones we identified when he deals with specific issues and questions in the Corinthian church. An awareness that unity, love, freedom, equality, and the presence of Spirit are integral to being in Christ guide Paul's responses in his pursuit, with the Corinthian Christians, of authentic manifestations of their Gospel response. The occasion for the apostle's written comments are questions the Corinthian's pose in their letter to him and information from oral reports. This section focuses on these concerns regarding immorality in Corinth, lifestyles, use of food offered to idols, roles in the community, use of gifts, and the collection, and it identifies the principles involved in Paul's responses.

Immorality and Lawsuits (1 Cor 5-6)

This particular section of Paul's letter sparked interest in Corinth not because of the issues themselves but because of the underlying emphasis on the importance of the body (Murphy-O'Connor, *1 Corinthians*, 39-54). Paul's view of the body differs from that of the Corinthians, who consider that physical actions have no moral significance. They would say: "Shun fornication! Every sin that a person commits is outside the body" (1 Cor 6:18a). To which Paul responds "but the fornicator sins against the body itself" (1 Cor 6:18b). While this section deals with sexual immorality in the form of incest (5:1-13), lawsuits among Christians (6:1-11), and sexuality immorality in terms of casual relations (6:12-20), similar principles underlie Paul's responses. He focuses on the importance of the physical body and the community as the body of Christ.

Paul boldly opens this section of the letter by identifying behavior that is a moral prohibition for both Jews and Gentiles. "It is actually reported that there is sexual immorality among you, and of a kind that is not found even among pagans; for a man is living with his father's wife" (1 Cor 5:1). The Corinthians take pride in their sexual freedom, but Paul calls them arrogant and boastful (1 Cor 5:2.6; 6:12). While Paul's letters often contain vice lists, he integrates specific situations in the Corinthian church into these lists (1 Cor 5:9-13; 6:9-11; 2 Cor 12:20-21). For the Christian community, baptism changes standards since "you were washed, you were sanctified, you were justified in the name of the

Lord Jesus Christ and in the Spirit of our God" (1 Cor 6:11). Likewise, Paul reminds the community that the body is for the Lord since they are members of Christ and share one spirit with him (1 Cor 6:13.15.17). Indeed, "your body is a temple of the Holy Spirit within you, which you have from God, and that you are not your own?" (1 Cor 6:19). In this last part of the section (6:12-20), the apostle shows the connection between present sexual immorality and the threat it brings to future resurrection. Clearly the Christian attitude toward the body differs from what seems to be the practice in Corinth. The body is the vehicle through which we actualize our commitment to the Lord.

While Paul rejects Corinthian views and behavior, judging the situation and calling for expulsion of the deviant member from the community (1 Cor 5:13), he also insists that the community itself deal with the issue (1 Cor 5:4-5.12) (Meeks 128). He clarifies a possible misunderstanding of his former teaching and focuses on responsibilities within the faith community (1 Cor 5:9-13).

Paul's assessment of litigation revolves around two points, the community should not be involved in disputes and, if these arise, the community is the place to deal with it. The apostle again draws out the implications between conduct and commitment to the Gospel. Within this short section we see Paul identifying a theological framework for dealing with issues in the church and Christian life. He willingly passes judgment when the community reneges on its responsibility, challenges their use of freedom, affirms the goodness of the body, and urges mutual responsibility and discernment in difficult situations within the church.

Lifestyles of the Corinthian Christians (1 Cor 7:1-40)

This section begins Paul's responses to the Corinthian's questions, addressing problems arising from social status in this chapter. The pattern is similar to the previous section in that Paul begins and ends with problems that are fundamentally sexual (1 Cor 7:1-16; 25-40), while dealing with circumcision and slavery (1 Cor 7:18-24) in between (Murphy-O'Connor, *1 Corinthians*, 58). The center section clarifies the principle at stake—"remain in the condition in which you were called" because social status has no relevance in the faith community (1 Cor 7:20).

"Now concerning the matters about which you wrote: 'It is well for a man not to touch a woman'" (1 Cor 7:1) indicates a Corinthian position noted by Paul from a previous letter; he then reacts to their position. To the modern reader, statements regarding the anxieties of the married (1 Cor 7:32-34), with no acknowledgment of the work of missionary couples or the role of hospitality in house churches, seem lopsided or absurd. Paul's statements regarding his personal preference for celibacy seem to disregard the Corinthian's thinking on the matter (1 Cor 7:7-8.25-26.36-38.40). According to commentators, the Corinthians probably regarded celibacy highly and marriage negatively (Hurd 166), so Paul reaffirms, "I think that, in view of the impending crisis, it is well for you to remain as you are" (1 Cor 7:26). Corinthian women seem to claim authority over their own bodies (1 Cor 7:4) and undergo "social struggle and self-determination" within the new community (Wire 93). However, Paul encourages traditional sexual behavior for women, limiting their newly expanded social roles and their freedom (Wire 114).

Within this section, Paul questions the directions chosen by the Christians in Corinth, even though he, himself, was the source of the original teaching (Barrett, *2 Corinthians*, 38-39). Perhaps, Paul understands the complexities and realities of life better than the church (Murphy-O'Connor, *1 Corinthians*, 76), but he continues to alienate students and readers with his disjointed comments.

Embedded within the chapter, however, are positive statements regarding the Lord's call (7:17) and mutual responsibility in relationships (7:4.13-14), plus a mild comment on slavery from a Christian perspective (7:24). Because of the Gospel, the status of women and slaves, in particular, changed in substantial ways. Paul seems to be placing limits on their freedom and equality by extolling the Lord's initial gifts to them and the status quo of social order.

Problems from the Corinthian Environment
(1 Cor 8:1-11:1)

While this section contains material of limited interest to the contemporary reader, Paul utilizes principles of perennial value, such as Christian freedom, conscience, and the believer's stance in a non-Christian environment. Paul's pattern is similar to the previous section in that the beginning and ending (1 Cor 8:1-13 and 10:23-11:1) speak of food sacrificed to idols, and the center section (9:1-10:22) offers some principles to address community questions (Murphy-O'Connor, *1 Corinthians*, 77). The term conscience (*syneidesis*), familiar to Stoics and Epicureans, becomes part of Christian vocabulary because of the apostle's usage (1 Cor 8:7.10.12; 10:25.27.28.29). In addition, Paul strongly states his own relationship to the law when he places the law of Christ above any other (1 Cor 9:20-21). The apostle quotes Corinthian slogans (1 Cor 8:1.4.8; 10:23) and identifies the positions of the strong and weak in relation to food to idols in the respective sections.

When Paul deals with the issue of conscience, he sets a context for his discussion. He does not see the buying or eating of idol meat as the issue (1 Cor 10:25), rather the relationship between people is what really matters. "Both the structure and the substance of Paul's response makes the effect of one's behavior on others the criterion of ethics" (Horsley, "Consciousness," 586). He writes: "But take care that this liberty of yours does not somehow become a stumbling block to the weak" (1 Cor 8:9). Interestingly, the solution to the problem is not the ethical issue; freedom of conscience is! (Horsley 574). What Paul attempts to do is cultivate principled ethical thinking by the Corinthians (Brunt 115). However, he insures the inclusion of faith, freedom, conscience, mutual responsibility, discernment, and love in the process, thereby avoiding simplistic solutions to a problem they encounter every day.

Another aspect of Paul's challenge in this section is the use of himself as an example of appropriate behavior. Paul readily adapts and accommodates himself to changing circumstances, sometimes being called inconsistent rather than principled (Richardson 360). However, after identifying the pattern of his approach to others (1 Cor 9:20-23), he cites the Gospel as his prime motivation (1 Cor 9:23). Perhaps the Corinthians neglect to bring a Christian perspective into their assessment of freedom and responsibility. How easy it is for us to do the same!

Problems in the Assembly (1 Cor 11:2-34)

In dealing with information from oral reports that indicates a disruption of unity and order in the community, Paul takes a hard stand on particular practices within the church. Although he begins with a commendation (1 Cor 11:2), the tone of this chapter is harsh and threatening (1 Cor 11:16-27.34). The issues of head coverings and meals distract from the tradition handed on regarding the Eucharist. However, we again observe Paul's pattern of response in this section on the Lord's Supper. Paul frames the words of institution of the Eucharist (1 Cor 11:23-26) with a critique of the situation in Corinth (1 Cor 11:17-22 and 27-34).

Why the consternation regarding women's head covering and proper dress in the assembly? The question has been asked and answered in a variety of ways (Wire 220-223). Is Paul speaking of authority over another when he uses "head" or "source" in his discussion (vss 3.5.6.10)? Is Paul opting for distinctions between women and men because of associations with homosexuality (vss 14-15)? Is the apostle seeking to limit the role of women prophets in the community (Wire 130)? Or does the context of worship suggest that lack of head covering for women distracts from the glory of God (vs 3) (Wire 121; Hooker, "Authority," 415)? We could go on!

What Paul does affirm is that both women and men exercise liturgical leadership in the Christian assembly and that both have gifts of prayer and prophecy. A Corinthian house church provides the context for these community celebrations and the utilization of the Spirit's gifts. Tension exists in these formative years as the church explores specific applications of the Gospel's message of freedom and equality. However, women in Corinth claim an authority to pray and prophesy publicly, an authority denied them in the synagogue but afforded in Christ (Hooker, "Authority," 410-416).

While Paul's real agenda is unknown from the text, he does affirm order and unity in the church. This principle underscores his concern for divisions evident during the meal (1 Cor 11:18-19), and he challenges the Corinthians to examine their behavior and discern their options (1 Cor 11:28-29). From the tone of the chapter, we can be fairly certain that Paul will further pursue the discussion since factions and disunity are a particular concern in the Corinthian church.

Use of Gifts of the Spirit (1 Cor 12-14)

This section continues with problems in the liturgical assembly and brackets the powerful teaching on love (1 Cor 13) with Paul's reflections on spiritual gifts (1 Cor 12 and 14). The text explicitly identifies the community as a body, with its many members constituted by the one Spirit (1 Cor 12:12-27). This understanding of church sets the theological tone for the entire section. Gifts of prophecy, speaking in tongues, and knowledge receive special attention in light of Corinth's situation (1 Cor 1:29; 2:12-13), and the emphasis on specific attitudes and attributes of love indicates lapses in the Corinthian church (1 Cor 13:1-2.4-6). Many commentators see the admonition regarding women's silence in the assembly (1 Cor 14:34-36), a contradiction to Paul's recognition of their roles in 1 Corinthians 11, as an insertion or interpolation by a later editor. Others identify the context for the admonition as a large assembly of several house churches in the area that requires order (Wire 229-232). The text itself conveys something of the flavor and excitement in the Corinthian church as it celebrates its new life in Christ.

Paul engages the community in its assessment of gifts by offering his own perspective on the value of *glossolalia* or speaking in tongues. "Nevertheless, in church I would rather speak five words with my mind, in order to instruct others also, than ten thousand words in a tongue" (1 Cor 14:19; cf 4:4-7; 14:22). While this gift enhances the social prestige of the recipient in the eyes of the community, Paul renders it useless unless interpretation occurs (1 Cor 14:13.27-28). In fact, the apostle challenges the church to desire the higher gifts and to utilize them, within the context of love, to build up the body and to witness to others (1 Cor 12:31; 14:1.3.5.12). Along with these principles for use of gifts, Paul affirms the variety of gifts, the unity of the body, and order in the assembly. He strongly suggests that Christians discern the best use of their gifts, and he questions the free expression of prophecy and tongues in the assembly. Obviously, Paul walks on shaky ground in relation to the Corinthian church, especially the women prophets! His reliance on love as the central ethical principle, however, is a unique insight that few would resent or resist.

The Collection for Jerusalem (1 Cor 16:1-4; 2 Cor 8-9)

In the closing chapter of 1 Corinthians, Paul deals with their question regarding the collection. "Now concerning the collection for the saints: you should follow the directions I gave to the churches of Galatia" (1 Cor 16:1). His points are clear—put something aside every week, and upon his arrival in Corinth, he will send letters with the individuals, approved by the church, to carry the gift to Jerusalem (1 Cor 16:2-4). While these directives sound administrative, as do sections in his later letter, the collection symbolizes the unity of Jewish and Gentile groups in the church. Paul develops his guidelines in 2 Corinthians, which some consider two independent letters, one to Corinth (2 Cor 8) and the other to the province of Achaia (2 Cor 9).

Scripture attests to sharing resources with the poor in the early church (Acts 2:45; 4:34-35), and the apostle identifies the example of other Pauline communities, such as Galatia and Macedonia, in these texts. More importantly, Paul suggests generosity and freedom as qualities for giving in response to need (2 Cor 8:2.3.13-14; 9:9.11). While the Corinthians have considerable financial resources, we know that a project like the Corinthian canal is beyond their means (Murphy-O'Connor, *Corinth*, 111), and their community reflects a cross-section in terms of status and wealth (1 Cor 1:26). However, Paul urges the community to think generously as a concrete manifestation of their love and unity in Christ. This kind of involvement instills a sense of mutual responsibility within the church, a quality Paul encourages in faith communities. For something as mundane as a collection, Paul summons his theological insight so that the community's great generosity "will produce thanksgiving to God" (2 Cor 9:11). What an example for our appeals to share resources in the church/world today!

While Paul deals with other theological and personal issues in the Corinthian correspondence, such as the meaning of the resurrection of the body and his own apostolic effectiveness, these enable us to identify how he applies principles and values to matters of community concern.

Dealing with Ethical Questions Today

Moral concerns, business and medical ethics, sexual morality, social responsibility, equality and justice in church and society are examples of issues mature Christians deal with every day. While the examples may change, the concreteness of the situations do not. "Dealing as they do with such mundane matters as sex, taxes, diet, lawsuits, circumcision, ecstatic speech and intramural squabbles, Paul's letters bear the unmistakable imprint of this world!" (Roetzel, *Letters*, 50). Not much of a case for generic homilies or classes!

More importantly, Paul sets forth a few principles for community discernment, such as the holiness of life, our equality in Christ, the unity of the body, and the witness of love. His understanding of freedom of conscience, with its relational perspective, forces the community to move away from simple solutions to complex issues. Although he offers advice and opinion, this persuasive minister respects the churches' ability to make their own decisions (Holmberg 81). "Nowhere does Paul employ guilt or recompense to God for past wrongs as motivations to moral action" (Sampley 101).

Personal responsibility, responsiveness to congregational issues, lived values within the community, and mutual respect seem to color his interaction with the church. While this sounds ideal, let us be mindful that the Corinthian church caused Paul more pain than comfort. His pastoral commitment and theological reflection, so evident in these letters, allow him to see the big picture while attending to the concerns of the day. How Paul deals with issues is more important than the issue itself—a point that often rings true in our own life and ministry.

Paul leaves us no set of principles for use in every situation, but he does identify perennial values that should mark our interactions and decisions. We see theology at work in the dynamic exchange between Paul and the Corinthian Christians. We continue the conversation and discernment, today, in our ministry.

For Personal and Group Reflection

1. The early church gathered in the homes of well-to-do Christians to share faith and celebrate as a community of believers. What is the value of meeting in homes for churches today?

2. The house churches provided the possibility for alternative structures, leadership, and lifestyles in the early church. How do family life and relationships affect your approach to ministry?

3. A sense of belonging to and participating in the life of church characterized the experience of the early Christians. In what ways do you develop this spirit in your local church?

4. Equality in relationships was a sign of the early church in terms of leadership, ministry, and responsibility. How do you see the principle of equality operative in the ministry of women in the local church? What are the gaps in the application of this principle in the contemporary church?

5. Paul used many images and metaphors to describe the church. How do you describe the community of believers? What

attributes do you emphasize in your description?

6. The community as the body of Christ is a favorite Pauline formulation that allows for unity and diversity in the church. How do your aims in ministry foster unity among believers and diversity in the community?

7. Paul identified the principles of unity, love, freedom, equality, and the presence of the Spirit in all as he dealt with difficult situations in the early church. What Christian principles do you use in your decision-making as an ecclesial minister? Why?

8. The Corinthian correspondence dealt with specific matters of concern to the local community. What are the issues you face as a minister in your community or parish? What values and principles do you affirm as you address these concerns?

9. Many of the problems Paul faced in Corinth originated in an environment that seemed to be at odds with Gospel values. How did Paul address freedom of conscience in the question of food to idols and use the principle of equality in the problems in the Christian assembly and the use of gifts? How do you deal with ethical dilemmas today?

10. The variety of gifts in the early church was a clear manifestation of the presence of the Spirit. What are the Spirit's gifts that you identify in yourself and in your community? How effectively are they utilized for building up the church?

Chapter Five

Liturgical Interests in the Corinthian Community

Accustomed as they were to celebration and worship in Corinth, it is not surprising to discover liturgical interests in Paul's letters to the Corinthians. The Isthmian games and the arrival of many visitors and speakers to the city offer occasions for festive gatherings (1 Cor 9:24-25). Numerous temples to gods and goddesses cultivate an atmosphere of ritual, worship, and sacrifice, as Paul notes in these letters (1 Cor 8:4-5.7; 10:18-20). The probable presence of a synagogue and Jewish households, such as those of Crispus and Sosthenes (1 Cor 1:1.14.16), expose the Corinthians to the Jewish Scriptures, festivals, and worship. Paul's use of Passover imagery and references to Moses and the law indicate the community's awareness of these celebrations as well as the apostle's teaching interests (1 Cor 5:6-8; 9:9; 10:1-11).

Gathering in households of faith provides Corinthians with the opportunity to celebrate in a distinctively Christian manner, and these occasions become a vital part of the early church's development. This setting is the framework for the creation of a Christian identity and the beginnings of its cultic and liturgical experiences. However, worship is not an isolated celebration. Paul connects worship with life using the term "spiritual worship" to connote this integration in his other letters (Rom 12:1-2). Consistent with his broad understanding of worship is his description of all believers as a holy people and the move away from "holy places and seasons, or holy acts" performed by designated holy persons on behalf of the congregation (Ridderbos 481).

The Corinthian community celebrates baptism, gathers together for meals, preaching, prayer, and Eucharist. The Corinthians believe that the presence of the Spirit, community need, and sense of church inspires those gifted by the Spirit to assume various roles and responsibilities in the assembly. References to forgiveness, reconciliation, prayer, and new life in these letters offer us a composite picture of liturgical and sacramental celebrations in the early church. As we read 1 and 2 Corinthians from the perspective of liturgy, we may register surprise at the simplicity of the beginnings of our Christian worship. Impressive, however, is the enthusiasm of the gatherings, the realistic context of the celebrations, and the possibilities offered in Scripture for other liturgical expressions and experiences.

Celebrations in the Corinthian Church

Celebration As Spiritual Worship

Worship of God is an opportunity for the early Christians to establish their own identity in their religiously diverse environment. In fact, believers in Corinth cultivate an understanding of themselves in relation to those outside in their community gatherings. We see in 1 and 2 Corinthians that Paul uses several designations for the group to convey a sense of identity and belonging. He writes to the church of God, called to be saints (1 Cor 1:2; 16:1; 2 Cor 1:1; 8:4; 13:12), and specifies that believers must have the mind of Christ (1 Cor 2:16). These brothers and sisters (1 Cor 1:10.26; 2:1; 3:1; 16:20; 2 Cor 13:11) are beloved children (1 Cor 4:14.17). As one body (1 Cor 10:17) and a new creation (2 Cor 5:17), God "establishes us with you in Christ and has anointed us, by putting his seal on us and giving us his Spirit in our hearts as a first installment" (2 Cor 1:21-22). These expressions reflect the special relationship between the members of this new family and their distinctiveness from others.

Contrasting terminology, often indicating separateness, also occurs in the Corinthian letters. Paul speaks of those outside the faith community (1 Cor 5:12; 9:21; 14:23) as unbelievers (1 Cor 6:6; 14:23; 2 Cor 6:14), wrongdoers (1 Cor 6:9), the separated, and unclean (1 Cor 7:14; 2 Cor 6:17). Furthermore, he believes the Gospel remains veiled for those who perish (2 Cor 4:3), while others continue to be part of the old covenant (2 Cor 3:14) or suffer condemnation with the world (1 Cor 11:32). As we listen to these descriptors, we can identify boundaries between Christians and those who do not share faith in Christ. The Corinthians celebrate these distinctions liturgically, and as believers they establish the parameters of their belief in their special communal gatherings.

While first-century Christians do not have such things as shrines, cult statues, temples, sacrifices, pilgrimages, or public festivals (Meeks 140), they have shared beliefs and shared language that express their beliefs, thereby promoting cohesiveness in the group (93). Liturgical celebrations, with their focus on belief, language, and ritual, continue to function in similar ways today. Distinctive aspects of ritual and worship create an atmosphere that binds a community together and expresses its identity.

When the Corinthian Christians come together, they most often share a meal together (1 Cor 11:17-18.20.33-34). However, expulsion of a member for deviant sexual behavior (1 Cor 5:4) also occurs in a gathering of believers. We know that Paul's letters, or sections of them, are read in the churches (1 Thess 5:27) and that people participate in the assembly with "a hymn, a lesson, a revelation, a tongue, or an interpretation...for building up" the faith community (1 Cor 14:26). The Corinthian letters offer examples of blessings (2 Cor 1:3-7), tongues and prophecy (1 Cor 14:2-12), instruction and admonition (1 Cor 14:3.19.31) as integral parts of the community celebrations. "Regular readings and homilies in the assemblies" are a likely occurrence as Christians gather together on a weekly basis (Meeks 146). Prayer is both spontaneous and according to custom and often ends with an "Amen" by the assembly (1 Cor 14:13-16). Greetings and a "holy kiss" are part of the celebration as the community enjoys its communion in the Lord (1 Cor 16:19-20; 2 Cor 13:12).

We begin to see the contours of liturgical celebrations taking shape in Corinth. But more important is the fact that every aspect of Corinthian life is part of their worship of the Lord. These letters and the issues they contain are integral to the spiritual worship of the community. "All members of the church have access to God (Rom 5:2) and a share in the Holy Spirit; all of life is service to God; there is no 'profane' area" (Ridderbos 481). What wonderful testimony to the holiness of life! While the celebrations define the community gathered together in the Lord's name, they do not exclude any person or any aspect of life from its worship. This realization of inclusiveness associated with worship accounts for the realistic tone and full participation of the community in Corinth. Perhaps revisiting this early tradition will enhance our contemporary liturgical celebrations and challenge us to think in terms of their connection to the daily life of the congregation.

Baptism: A Celebration of Transformation

All of us have images of baptism in our minds—a child, water, light, oil, pouring, lighting, anointing, clothing, parents, godparents, community, priest. We can recall the specialness of the celebration in the gatherings of family and friends that usually follow the church ceremony. In one such gathering of a Tongan family, my husband and I were asked to share what the child's baptism meant to us as godparents. Then each person present reflected on the meaning of the event for themselves and the family. What a marvelous expression of faith and commitment! What does our celebration of the sacrament have in common with baptismal celebrations in the Corinthian church? Unfortunately, Paul does not describe the ritual in his letters, but he does offer an understanding of the significance of this event.

References to Baptism in the Corinthian Correspondence

Paul's initial statement regarding baptism occurs early in 1 Corinthians when he speaks of those he did, and did not, baptize (1 Cor 1:14-16). He then reflects on his own commissioning and sets a framework for understanding baptism. "For Christ did not send me to baptize but to proclaim the gospel, and not with eloquent wisdom, so that the cross of Christ might not be emptied of its power" (1 Cor 1:17). For Paul, the preaching of the Gospel, apprehended by faith, provides the context for baptism (Banks 82). Furthermore, God gives "baptism its power, on the faith of the one baptized" (Ridderbos 411). Paul establishes a relationship between baptism and faith. As we read these passages, we probably question our tradition of infant baptism, since the Corinthian experience is the baptism of adults and of households who profess belief in the Gospel. In our ceremonies, we substitute the faith of family and community for the faith of the child. Although immersion into the water was probably customary in the early church, our practice differs. Third-century artistic depictions in the catacombs that show water being poured over the head probably account for some of our rituals (Meeks 151).

Other references in the Corinthian letters indicate aspects of the community's experience of baptism. "And this is what some of you used to be. But you were washed, you were sanctified, you were justified in the name of the Lord Jesus Christ and in the Spirit of our God" (1 Cor 6:11). This passage is rich in significance because it contrasts the Corinthians' previous state with their present state, referring to the transformational change rendered by this rite of initiation. For the Corinthian church, baptism becomes a boundary-setting ritual (Meeks 102). Paul identifies a basic theological insight when he describes baptism as a cleansing that brings salvation through Christ. The further connection between baptism and the Spirit suggests the scope of fulfillment and transformation that Christians can expect in their lives as a result of this sacrament.

In 2 Corinthians, Paul makes his only reference to anointing in his letters. "But it is God who establishes us with you in Christ and has anointed us" (2 Cor 1:21). While documentation of the association of anointing and baptism occurs only in the second century, many commentators see this passage in a baptismal context (Furnish 148-150). We include anointing in our ceremonies today.

Paul uses other formulations in the Corinthian letters to remind the community of their baptismal commitment (1 Cor 8:6; Murphy-O'Connor, *1 Corinthians*, 80), and he often employs language reminiscent of baptism (2 Cor 3:16-18; 4:4-6) (Kim 142). Paul's only reference to baptism on behalf of the dead (1 Cor 15:29) may reflect a Corinthian practice, for stranger things happened in Corinth! Since baptism is "a powerful proclamation of death and resurrection" (Barrett, *1 Corinthians*, 364), Paul may use this statement to reflect his sufferings on behalf of those who are spiritually dead (Murphy-O'Connor, *1 Corinthians*, 144).

The baptismal formula located within Paul's discussion of spiritual gifts in the body of Christ is very important to the Corinthian's understanding of baptism. "For in the one Spirit we were all baptized into one body—Jews or Greeks, slaves or free—and we were all made to drink of one Spirit" (1 Cor 12:13; cf Gal 3:28; Col 3:10-12; Gen 1:27-28; 5:1-2). While the Corinthian formula omits the designation of male and female in the Galatian passage, the text concurs that baptism is "the event whereby people of radically different backgrounds are inaugurated into the unifying reality of the body of Christ" (Carlson 260). Thus, the community accepts social distinctions but integrates them into Christ through whom we share the one Spirit (Wire 138). Interestingly, Paul by-passes Jewish circumcision as the rite of initiation, considering it irrelevant to Christians (Fiorenza, *Memory*, 221). Focusing on the role of the Spirit in relation to baptism is an insight Paul offers in this passage.

The Ritual of Baptism

While we know little of the form of baptismal rituals in Corinth, the texts affirm a water bath, probably immersion into the water, that had precedent in the Jewish rites of purification (Meeks 150). Allusions to the old and new human suggest the taking off and putting on of clothing. The confession of faith may have been as simple as a proclamation of Jesus as Lord or variations of the formulas that convey equality in Christ. The testimony to ritual action is sparse in the Corinthian text, and so we can only surmise the components of the celebration in the Corinthian church.

The Meaning of Baptism for the Corinthian Christians

Baptism confirms the faith of the Corinthian believer and establishes a right relationship between the believer and God. However, Paul sees it as only the beginning of a process of transformation in Christ. Baptism also implies inauguration into a community of believers and communion with the brothers and sisters of the Lord. This body of Christ or new creation witnesses to its life in the Spirit, a significant aspect for the Corinthian community. Because of the cleansing waters of baptism and empowerment by the Spirit, Christian believers stand in contrast to those outside the community of faith. Paul draws out specific distinctions in attitude and lifestyle throughout 1 and 2 Corinthians. Underlying Paul's understanding of baptism in these letters (1 Cor 1:13), but explicit elsewhere (Rom 5:3-6), is the Christian's incorporation into the death of Christ. In fact, Christ's death gives meaning to the rite of baptism (Carlson 258-259), and Paul frequently preaches on the implications of this reality to the Corinthian church.

The Corinthian correspondence attests in some way to the baptismal traditions handed down to us in the Scriptures. These traditions associate baptism with water, the Spirit, and the presence of gifts (1 Cor 6:11; 12:13). They include descriptions of leaving off the old humanity and putting on Christ (1 Cor 12:12-13) and Christian participation in the dying and rising of Christ, a unifying thought underlying the Corinthian text (2 Cor 4:7-14) (Wire 167-168).

Baptism means transformation in relationships within the community of faith and in the new freedom the Corinthian church experiences in Christ. Life becomes radically different for these Christians because of their baptism. While the Corinthian letters do not speak of many aspects of the rite of baptism that we celebrate today, they do challenge us to see this incorporation into Christ as the basis of our life and the foundation of our ministry.

The Christian Assembly: A Celebration of Community

Paul speaks of the gathering of the church in a number of places in 1 Corinthians, and specifies the existing divisions and some inappropriate behavior in the community (11:17-18.22.33; 14:23.26.40). These abuses concern Paul because they are incompatible with his understanding of the body of Christ. In addition, the outsiders present will have a skewed picture of the Christian assembly—"will they not say that you are out of your mind?" (1 Cor 14:23). Concern for dress, for proper use of gifts, and for order in church in these sections of the Corinthian correspondence should not distract us from discovering the exciting testimony we have regarding the Christian assembly. Paul's emphasis on community throughout 1 and 2 Corinthians attests to the importance of these gatherings of the households of faith, and their struggles allow us to see the difficulties of creating an alternative environment within the religious and societal milieu of the period.

Essential Elements in the Gatherings of the Households of Faith

Paul mentions both traditions and customs as he addresses the Christians in Corinth (1 Cor 11:2.16.23), indicating that the churches share some components of belief and practice among various communities. Repeated comments about the place of food and the sharing of a meal together show how central this experience is to the assembly of Christians (1 Cor 8, 10, 11). These dinner celebrations provide the occasion to remember the Lord's Supper and to share the Spirit's gifts for the upbuilding of the church (1 Cor 14). The Corinthian church certainly celebrates with food and drink in households large enough for gathering the diverse members of the community together.

This meal is an opportunity to witness to the unity of the church (1 Cor 10:17; 11:18); to pray, prophesy, and speak in tongues (1 Cor 11:4-5; 14:1-40); and to offer "a hymn, a lesson, a revelation" for the edification of the community (1 Cor 14:26). The proclamation of the Word assumes a variety of forms in Corinth, and blessings, thanksgivings, and expressions such as "Amen" and "Maranatha" are part of the communal celebration (Meeks 159). We also know that Paul does not make distinctions between clergy, laity, or ministers as we do today, nor does he explicitly mention special leaders in the Christian assembly (Banks 133; Branick 92). In the Corinthian church, the head of household presides at the gathering, and these leaders are both women and men. The liturgical celebration itself, however, is the responsibility of the whole community and, as the Corinthian letters indicate, liturgy assumes a variety of forms that invite participation according to gift.

While we can identify with many aspects of these assemblies of the community, Paul's letters to the church in Corinth challenge us to rethink essential components in our liturgical celebrations. Our responses to questions regarding the who, how, why, where, and when of Christian communal celebrations must take into account the earliest biblical testimony as well as later traditions handed on in the church.

The Spirit of the Christian Assembly

Reading the liturgical sections of 1 Corinthians allows us to sense the quality and tone of the worship experiences in this early Christian community. The family setting contributes to the intimacy and friendliness of the gathering, while the sharing of food creates a festive atmosphere. In addition, a common meal indicates the mutual commitment of the participants and contributes to their growth as a faith community. "Thus the meal that they shared together not only reminded the members of their relationship with Christ and one another but actually deepened it, much as participation in a common meal by family or group not only symbolizes but really cements the bond between them" (Banks 86).

The tone of the assembly is one of excitement and spontaneity, particularly in the manifestations of the gifts of the Spirit. While Paul calls the actions of women prophets into question, their presence and activity contribute to the sense of enthusiasm in the community. Likewise, the participation of all members according to gift, not in officially designated roles, is a sign of the transition to a new creation in Christ. Distinctions between individual household gatherings and larger assemblies of churches allow for diversity in the form of the celebration. The call for order deemed appropriate by the writer for larger gatherings, differs from the actual experience of the community indicated by the Corinthian texts. We glimpse the energy, spark, and creativity of new converts in the Christian assembly, a reminder to us of the joy of liturgical celebration.

Realistic as well as ecstatic experiences are part and parcel of the assemblies in Corinth. Food preparation and distribution, clashes between various social groups, struggles to understand the proper use of spiritual gifts, and the acceptance of women in their new roles contribute to the difficulties Paul addresses in these letters. This touch of realism easily translates into comparable situations in the church today. However, while Paul exhorts the community to improve the quality of its life and its celebrations, he also focuses on essential aspects of unity in the body and mutual love. Perhaps, his perspective is of help to us as we deal with the practicalities of liturgical worship. The Christian assembly is a celebration of the community, and the growth of any Christian community is complex, painful, and slow.

The Lord's Supper:
A Celebration of the Lord's Presence

The Corinthian correspondence offers us the earliest indication of important features regarding the celebration of the Lord's Supper (1 Cor 11:17-34). Specific references identify the context of Eucharist as the basic act of eating a common meal (1 Cor 11:21; 10:21). The ritual actions are an imitation of the meal Jesus shared with his disciples on the night before he died, when he broke and distributed bread, offered thanksgiving, and said "Do this in remembrance of me" (1 Cor 11:23-24). The celebration has a vicarious meaning, "for you" (1 Cor 11:24), and it contains an eschatological dimension, "until he comes" (1 Cor 11:26) (Meeks 158-159).

Paul's account is the earliest tradition we have available to us, and it is closest in language and theology to Luke's account (Lk 22:15-20; cf Mk 14:22-25; Mt 26:26-29) that comes some thirty years later. Repetition of the action as remembrance (1 Cor 11:24-25) is an addition by the apostle in light of the Corinthian's inability to see the connection between past and present. "What he desires to evoke is the active remembrance of total commitment to Christ which makes the past real in the present, thus releasing a power capable of shaping the future" (Murphy-O'Connor, *1 Corinthians*, 112). Paul also writes of the Lord's Supper in 1 Corinthians 10:14-22, where he contrasts the celebration to other sacrifices and relates it to the church's identity as the body of Christ. "The cup of blessing that we bless, is it not a sharing in the blood of Christ? The bread that we break, is it not a sharing in the body of Christ? Because there is one bread, we who are many are one body, for we all partake of the one bread" (1 Cor 10:16-17).

Ritual Actions in the Corinthian Celebration of Eucharist

The Corinthian text offers us a few indications of the actions associated with the eucharistic celebration. The setting is the sharing of a meal, and Paul uses images from this familiar celebration. We notice the explicit mention of the "cup of blessing that we bless" and partaking "of the one bread" at "the table of the Lord" (1 Cor 10:16.21). Drinking the cup of the Lord and eating the bread become the ritual actions of the celebration in Corinth.

The text containing the words of institution (1 Cor 11:23-26) indicates further acts of giving thanks before breaking the bread and sharing the cup. Paul includes words that remind the community of the significance of the actions—it is "the new covenant in my blood" that the community celebrates "in remembrance" of the Lord. "For as often as you eat this bread and drink the cup, you proclaim the Lord's death until he comes" (1 Cor 11:26). These words and actions include references to the Jewish Scriptures, its sacrifices, meal celebrations, and Passover feast (Dt 12:11-12; 18:1-4; Mal 1:7-12; Ezek 24:5-8; 41:22; 44:16; Isa 55:11; Jer 31:31; Ex 12:14; 24:3-8).

If we include some of the rituals associated with meals and Sabbath observances in this period, such as the welcome of guests, washing of feet, greeting of a kiss, readings, and so on, we can identify a first-century basis for our celebrations of the Lord's Supper. For believers in Corinth, repetition of these words and acts solidifies their identification with the Lord and each other, as does our reenactment. But, our use of the ritual today contains the added dimension of remembering the early Christians and our ancestors throughout the centuries. Paul also reminds his community and us of our roots in Judaism through Jesus' words and in the rituals of the celebration itself. The rituals of the Lord's Supper became more stylized in form when separated from the context of a meal. A synod of Laodicea, held sometime between 360 and 370 CE, forbade the celebration of the Eucharist in the home, and this establishes the tradition known to us of worship in churches.

The Meaning of the Eucharistic Celebration

The celebration of the Lord's Supper in the Corinthian church is a celebration of Christ's presence within the community of believers. Paul sees it as a celebration of unity, commitment, and mutual love. The quality of communion among believers is integral to an authentic celebration of Eucharist, for Paul understands the body of Christ as inclusive of Christians (Ellis, "Soma," 141). The challenges of Paul to the Corinthians indicate his theological perspective—the sign of the real presence of the Lord is his body when it reflects its union with the Lord in its mutual love.

By remembering the words and acts of Jesus on the night before he died, Paul emphasizes the sacrificial aspects of the celebration. However, the sacrifice of Jesus is the great salvific event in which God acts on our behalf. We celebrate our faith in this worship service, just as the Corinthians celebrated their faith within the context of a shared meal. The Lord's Supper, however, is not only a reminder of a past event, the community celebrates it in the present, in anticipation of future glory. Paul mentions abuses within the meal in 1 Corinthians because of their intimate connection to the meaning of the celebration. He does not focus on the ritual action and format since these observances are rather fluid in this early period.

The essence of the Lord's Supper is a celebration of Christ's presence. His presence in the Christian assembly suggests a focus for our liturgies today. The community offers glory to God when it eats the bread and drinks from the cup worthily. As presiders and ministers of the Eucharist, we must assist the community in the discernment of its worthiness to celebrate at the Lord's table (1 Cor 11:27-29). This discernment should be along the lines of the quality of Christian life in the community. Perhaps we need this change in focus when we speak of the real presence of the Lord for Paul's emphasis is realistic, communal, and far simpler than later theology would have us believe.

Reconciliation: A Celebration of Peace

Although we find no references to a sacramental celebration of reconciliation in the Corinthian correspondence, we do discover key insights into Paul's understanding of God's action on our behalf. After speaking of the new creation, the apostle states: "All this is from God, who reconciled us to himself through Christ, and has given us the ministry of reconciliation; that is, in Christ God was reconciling the world to himself, not counting their trespasses against them, and entrusting the message of reconciliation to us" (2 Cor 5:18-19). The tradition emphasizes that God initiates the gracious act of reconciling the world, thereby establishing a renewed relationship between divinity and humanity. This reconciliation occurs through Christ who "For our sake he made him to be sin who knew no sin, so that in him we might become the righteousness of God" (2 Cor 5:21). Paul's unique use of the term "reconciliation" to indicate a transformation in the relationship between God and humankind indicates the new order established in Christ. While not always interchangeable with justification, reconciliation clearly "emphasizes that God's saving power is essentially the power of his love" (Furnish 336). The apostle suggests that something wonderful happened in Christ, but something more needs to be done. "So we are ambassadors for Christ, since God is making his appeal through us; we entreat you on behalf of Christ, be reconciled to God" (2 Cor 5:20). We must enter into the on-going process of reconciliation by opening our hearts to God's gift and by proclaiming the word of reconciliation through our lives and ministry. Nothing magical occurs, for Paul understands the freedom we each have to choose our response to the Lord.

The human condition itself creates a need for reconciliation among believers. Surprisingly, Paul rarely speaks of forgiveness of sins in his letters, preferring "sin" rather than "sins" (Bornkamm 151). He assumes that the Corinthians understand his views of sin, as the negative orientation of society—sin in the world; as their own choice of unauthentic existence—personal sin; and as manifestations in opposed groups in society—social sin. Paul is keenly aware that sin often prevails and that the Corinthian church acts under the power of sin. However, he is also convinced that we are responsible for our personal choices and must take responsibility for sin in our world. To speak only of the forgiveness of individual sins would be to trivialize Paul's understanding.

While he acknowledges the pervasiveness of sin, Paul understands that Christ assumed our human condition so that we "might become the righteousness of God" (2 Cor 5:21). Even his use of vice lists in these letters (1 Cor 5:10-11; 6:9-10) demonstrates the radical difference between the old and new creation that God effects through Christ. He also sees forgiveness itself as an act of the community, and Paul affirms its decision to forgive another (2 Cor 2:10). At times, Paul challenges the community to take radical steps to force a sinful member to repent (1 Cor 6:13), but he also speaks of a compassionate and loving response toward those who err (2 Cor 2:5-8). The atmosphere of forgiveness, reconciliation, and love is an essential part of the Christian community, and Paul emphasizes this point within the Letter of Reconciliation (2 Cor 1-9) because of his own difficulties with the Corinthian church. His focus offers us insight into the essence of a reconciled community that enables us to celebrate the sacrament more authentically.

According to the Corinthian correspondence, reconciliation is both a divine reality and a human need. We celebrate God's transformational action in Christ by our recognition that we are reconciled to God, just as the Corinthian Christians did. We, like they, are new creation, and this conviction must underlie every aspect of Christian life. However, just as the Corinthians were in need of reconciliation with Paul and among themselves, we too must work toward new levels of unity and harmony. Reconciliation means the acceptance of the peace and love of God as a gift and a power in our

Christian lives, and so we embrace the process of being reconciled (Ridderbos 184).

While 1 and 2 Corinthians offer us no rituals of reconciliation, these letters firmly establish that the celebration of new relationship with God through Christ is part and parcel of Christian life. Acknowledgment of sin and the need for forgiveness also constitute the Corinthian experience, and these realities demand recognition by believers. For the Christians in Corinth, the ministry of reconciliation is the task of all believers, and they understand that peace comes with faith in the Lord. Paul's letters also acknowledge the communal context for celebrating God's reconciling love and forgiveness and the Corinthian's forgiving actions. Certainly the changes in our contemporary celebrations of the sacrament resonate with the experience of the church in Corinth. The present emphasis within the sacrament of reconciliation is broader than individual sins; the context is community acknowledgment of its mutual responsibility for love and forgiveness. Our contemporary celebration relies less on ritual and more on the creation of a new spirit of unity and harmony. Our celebration of reconciliation is a celebration of peace, and in this aspect it mirrors the understanding Paul shares with the Corinthian church.

Resurrection Hope: A Celebration of New Life

No ritual for the final transition from physical death to newness of life exists in the letters to Corinth. However, the Corinthian Christians probably "buried their dead in the same places and in the same fashion as their neighbors," and the "commonest memorial rite was a meal in honor of the departed, often around a table-shaped stone in the cemetery, on several specific anniversaries of the day of death" (Meeks, *Urban*, 162). Despite the lack of documentation of detailed rituals, we do have an early recounting of the tradition of the resurrection in 1 Corinthians 15, and here we can discover the hopes and expectations of the early church.

"For I handed on to you as of first importance what I in turn had received: that Christ died for our sins in accordance with the scriptures, and that he was buried, and that he was raised on the third day in accordance with the scriptures" (1 Cor 15:3-4). While Paul handed on the tradition, he acknowledges that the Corinthians think otherwise about resurrection of the dead. "Now if Christ is proclaimed as raised from the dead, how can some of you say there is no resurrection of the dead?" (1 Cor 15:12). Paul connects Christ's resurrection to that of Christians and to their lifestyle (1 Cor 15:32). He speaks of change from perishable to imperishable existence, from a mortal body to immortality, and from death to victory, not only indicating a reversal of our present condition but our future transformation as well. In light of the Corinthians disdain for the body and their understanding of transformation as already full and complete, Paul's testimony challenges the faith and hope of the Corinthian church. He speaks of a mystery foreign to the understanding of many in the community who believe they already experience the full liberating aspects of Christ's resurrection.

Notice Paul's perspective in the Corinthian text. He stretches the Corinthian imagination beyond their present level of faith to the possibilities of further transformation in the future. While his arguments and logic are not of interest to us here, they in effect persuade the Corinthian community to celebrate their faith with a new element of hope. However wonderful their present experience, the fullness of time is still ahead of these Christians. "In a moment, in the twinkling of an eye, at the last trumpet. For the trumpet will sound, and the dead will be raised imperishable, and we will be changed" (1 Cor 15:52).

With this emphasis on hope comes the realization that any celebration of our transition at death must include the mystery of what we have not seen or heard. However, Paul understands that continuity, as well as discontinuity, exists between this age and the age to come, and the resurrected body will reflect both similarity and transformation (Ellis, "Soma," 142). Celebrating this dual dimension liturgically requires imagination and faith. Likewise, Paul challenges the Corinthian church to consider the ways resurrection hope affects their daily lives (1 Cor 15:30-32.58). When he reflects on his apostolic sufferings, he often connects these struggles in ministry to his hope of resurrection (2 Cor 4:7-5:10). The pain of loss has meaning in light of Paul's reminders to the

Corinthian church. The images he uses of death/life, earthly tent/heavenly dwelling, affliction/glory, unclothed/clothed, temporary/eternal offer us vivid contrasts that suggest consolation and hope as we deal with death (2 Cor 4:7-5:1). Although we lack a ritual from the early church for this ultimate transformation, the Corinthian letters offer a theological perspective for our celebration of new life.

Prayer and Life: A Celebration of Presence

The language of prayer permeates Paul's writings, and specific indications of prayer underscore its importance for the community of believers. In the Corinthian correspondence we can identify prayers of thanksgiving (1 Cor 1:4-7; 2 Cor 1:3-7), blessings (1 Cor 16:13.22; 2 Cor 13:9), and request (2 Cor 1:11; 12:8-10; 13:7). These examples of prayer focus on growth in faith, the quality of Christian life, and effectiveness in ministry (H. and L. Doohan, *Prayer*, 51-55). Paul also stresses attitudes in prayer that open us to a new experience of God and involve the whole person (1 Cor 14:13-15). Furthermore, he sees prayer as integral to Christian growth and maturity for the Christians in Corinth (1 Cor 3:2; 13:9-12; 2 Cor 13:9). While Paul's prayer remains simple, direct, and related to the Corinthian situation, he mentions a profound personal experience of prayer when he responds to challenges from his opponents (2 Cor 12:1-10). Unlike his other references to prayer, Paul relates something of the experience itself and omits its impact on his own life and ministry.

The Corinthian correspondence offers primary examples of *the church at prayer*. When the assembly of Christians gathers together, it offers prayers, hymns, instruction, tongues, and interpretation, aware of the Lord's presence in their midst (1 Cor 14:26). Celebrations of baptism that signify incorporation into Christ and the Christian community take place within the assembly of the Lord (1 Cor 6:11; 12:13.27). The great liturgical prayer of Eucharist takes place around the table of the Lord when the community gathers for prayer and remembrance (1 Cor 11:23-26). The Corinthian Christians share prayer, and its prayer emerges from its lived experience (1 Cor 10:31); "as you also join in helping us by your prayers, so that many will give thanks on our behalf for the blessing granted us through the prayers of many" (2 Cor 1:11). Interestingly, both prayer and liturgical leadership in these ecclesial gatherings result from the gifts of the Spirit (1 Cor 14:12-15:26). For Paul, prayer implies openness to new gifts of the Spirit and empowering others to live more authentically as church.

Finally, *prayer is a manifestation of the Spirit* within us, and the Spirit stimulates our prayer and deepens our union (1 Cor 6:17; 12:6.13) (H. and L. Doohan, *Prayer*, 135-143). In the Corinthian correspondence Paul consistently mentions the desired outcome of the Spirit's presence and gifts as building up the community of faith. These charisms, as prayer itself, result in the service of others. For Paul, ministry is the concrete expression of Christian spirituality and prayer. While the Corinthian church prays and prophesies spontaneously, according to the Spirit's gifts, Paul himself downplays ecstatic expressions of prayer. We find little mention of the mystical experience of prayer, of special places for prayer, or for well-designed formulas of prayer. However, a contemplative stance in the presence of God underlies the testimony and prayers we have in the Corinthian letters. Authentic Christian existence, growth in faith, living as church, and maturing in Christ are the focus and substance of prayer that the apostle emphasizes for this church. Paul and the Corinthian community consistently offer their prayer to God through Christ. In their prayer, they open themselves to change and celebrate the Lord's presence. Through prayer they draw on the abiding presence of the Lord to energize them in their life and ministry.

Paul's perspective on prayer and the prayers within 1 and 2 Corinthians offer us many insights into the *integration of prayer*, life, worship, and ministry. Our liturgical celebrations must include prayer that enhances our ability to celebrate the Lord's presence in all aspect of life and human relationship. Rhythms of prayer and quiet, the use of various kinds of prayer, the cultivation of prayerful attitudes, and appropriate challenges to personal as well as communal prayer are as important for contemporary Christians as they were for the Corinthian church. Only then will prayer permeate our daily lives and allow us to continually celebrate the presence of God.

Other Celebrations in the Corinthian Community

While the Corinthian letters only specify baptism and the Lord's Supper as liturgical celebrations of the community in this early period of church life, we know that groups celebrated various other aspects of their life transitions within the context of a meal or a gathering. These celebrations probably included occasions of marriage, death, and burial (Meeks 162-163). Rituals were important to the community as was the cultivation of its identity as believers. The lack of documentation, however, should not obscure the interests of the Corinthian community that could lead to a variety of communal celebrations. In addition, religious festivals, civic memorials, and family milestones would be reasons to celebrate both then and now (L. Doohan, *Mission*, 111-114; 122-127). A vivid and impressive example is the American celebration of Thanksgiving Day around our dinner tables and in our churches, with its remembrance of God's providential care of the early settlers symbolized in the bountiful harvest. Liturgical celebrations that have a ring of authenticity and spontaneity seem to need little persuasion to observe. The Corinthians experienced these moments in their lives, and we need to do the same. Cultural, ethnic, and religious diversity can lead to numerous modes of celebration. Sensitivity to the real calls to celebration in our personal and family situations will enrich our liturgical lives and open us to new approaches that will link worship and life as Paul urged in the Corinthian church.

For Personal and Group Reflection

1. Celebration is at the heart of the Christian experience. Paul saw all life as integral to the worship of the community. How do you celebrate life in your own families? How do you express gratitude and thanksgiving for

the gifts of God in creation, relationships, work, and society?

2. The Corinthian church celebrated many aspects of their faith life through gatherings, ritual, and prayer together. What aspects of Christian life do you celebrate as people of faith? Are there other moments of life that should or could be celebrated liturgically?

3. Baptism is a celebration of new life in Christ. How do you celebrate this sacrament as a faith community in your parish and family? What symbols of new life mark your rituals?

4. Baptism begins a new relationship with the community of faith. How do the rituals you celebrate symbolize these new relationships?

5. Christians gathered as a community of believers to manifest their unity in faith through sharing a meal and prayer. How do your eucharistic gatherings reflect the participation of the whole community and contribute to its growth?

6. The celebration of the Lord's Supper was intimately connected to life in the community. How do you build up the body of Christ through your ministry as well as through your celebration?

7. The Corinthian church understood its need for reconciliation, and Paul even described his ministry in terms of reconciliation. What are the manifestations of inauthentic existence on a personal, social, and world level that call for this celebration of peace today?

8. Liturgy often marks transitions in life. What are significant expressions of ritual and worship, in your experience, that mark the Christian's death and resurrection in Christ?

9. Prayer was integral to life and ministry for Paul and the early church. What prayer experiences do you find most significant in your personal life and as a faith community?

10. Liturgical celebrations differ because of culture, religious traditions, and personal history. How do you incorporate ethnic diversity and social traditions into your liturgies?

Chapter Six

The Ministry of Disciples in the Corinthian Letters

The Corinthian letters provide us with an energetic account of life in the early church. Because of the prolific correspondence between Paul and this Christian community, we are not only able to identify Paul's theological foundations for ministry, significant issues of mutual concern, and liturgical interests in Corinth, but also to see something of their development over a span of approximately seven years. The tone and spirit of dialogue in the letters permit an assessment of evolving relationships in the community, and 2 Corinthians 10-13, with its focus on Paul's apostolic defense, forces us to rethink any idealistic images we may have of the beginnings of our church. Particularly significant for educators and adult Christians today is Paul's focus on discipleship, mission, and ministry. These themes bring together many elements from our previous reflections in this book and examine other dimensions of the Corinthians' commitment, and ours too.

From its beginning Christianity was a missionary movement, involving all believers, to some degree, in the service and spread of the Gospel. The Corinthian letters reveal the deep commitment of Paul and the coworkers to ministry in Corinth and beyond, offering us a glimpse of the enthusiasm and energy of Christ's first-century disciples. Paul's own call to believe in the Gospel includes an understanding of his responsibility to minister in the Lord's name as apostle to the Gentiles. Whether as disciples or apostles, early Christians embrace their role in the mission of the church in outreach, support, and witness. Corinthian households become part of a network of hospitality, preaching, and information for Paul and the coworkers on their missionary journeys. Paul's letters establish links between the churches and foster unity by their content and exhortations. While the apostle's emphasis is on the local church, his approach as a missionary soon leads to a sense of interconnectedness among the widespread Christian communities. Paul refers to the faith of other churches in the Corinthian letters (1 Cor 1:2), includes places and people from different churches in his correspondence (1 Cor 16:1.5; 2 Cor 9:2-4), and ends his letters with greetings from individuals known to the various communities (1 Cor 16:17-19; Rom 16).

As an apostle Paul cultivates both a sense of independence, by supporting himself through a combination of manual work and missionary activity, and interdependence, by his reliance on coworkers and communities to share in the spread of the Gospel. In 1 and 2 Corinthians he identifies the qualities of the true apostle, such as knowledge, humility, and love (2 Cor 11:6-7.11), as a rebuttal to the accusations of his opponents. Likewise, Paul's boasting in the correspondence makes sense in light of the underlying tension and conflict between founder and church. We get the distinct impression that he is clearly on the defensive in 2 Corinthians. Although Paul's view of authentic ministry contradicts the approach of his opponents, his perspective offers a solid foundation for disciples today. The call for imitation of himself sounds strange to our ears, but Paul believes he mirrors Christ in his attitude and service, something others should do as well.

Living out the call to discipleship is challenging in any age, and Paul deftly describes the paradoxes of Christian life for this Spirit-filled community. Thus, Paul argues in Corinth that the believer's lifestyle should be a sign of contradiction to the values of the world. Wisdom and folly, power and weakness, shame and honor provide the hard lessons on discipleship for the Corinthian church. God's action in

Christ reverses the wisdom of this world and challenges all Christians to discern the real meaning of the Gospel for their unique situations.

Reading 1 and 2 Corinthians from the perspective of mission and ministry enables us to identify the essential components of discipleship. Building up the community of faith and partnership in mission are integral to the testimony of the Corinthian letters. Whether in Corinth or beyond, the ministry of disciples in this early period offers a new paradigm embodied in the relationship of apostle and coworkers in the church. Although these Christians struggle to live out equality in Christ, their strong faith conviction translates into partnership for the sake of the Gospel. Our present hope for a discipleship of equals within the church rests on the strong foundation of our earliest tradition. In addition, our emphasis on the ministry of all the baptized resonates with the testimony of the Corinthian correspondence.

Disciples, Apostles, and Missionaries in 1 and 2 Corinthians

Paul's Understanding of Call and Mission

As Paul begins his letters to the Corinthian church, he acknowledges his own call to be an apostle and the Corinthians' call to be saints with other believers in Jesus (1 Cor 1:1-2; 2 Cor 1:2). The reality of God's call and grace has implications for those who, like Paul, proclaim the Gospel (1 Cor 1:17.21.23; 2:4; 3:5.10). Those involved in such ministry are servants (1 Cor 3:5) who are "sent from God and stand in his presence" (2 Cor 2:17). In these letters, Paul reminds the Corinthian Christians that they are a new creation empowered by the Spirit because of their union with Christ. Discipleship, thus, becomes the equivalent of Christian life with its inclusive and transformational dimensions. As apostolic founder of the church in Corinth (1 Cor 4:15), Paul reminds the Corinthians of his call and theirs when necessary for exhortation or teaching (Kim 29). He authenticates the Gospel he proclaims by establishing his own apostolic call (Schmithals 38).

Paul integrates mission and ministry into his understanding of the call to discipleship. Paul attributes his own apostolic call, his understanding of the Gospel, and his mission to the Gentiles to God's revelation to him in the Damascus experience (Gal 1:12-16; 1 Cor 15:7-11; 2 Cor 4:6; 11:5). The prophetic calls of Jeremiah and Isaiah provide a foundation for Paul's interpretation of his call in terms of mission (Jer 1:1-5; Isa 6:1-13). Furthermore, the model of Jesus as servant of others and proclaimer of the kingdom of God challenges all Christians to imitate Christ (1 Cor 11:1). Paul witnesses to his faith by word and by example, just as Jesus and the prophets did before him. We do the same as we become models of commitment for others.

Paul realizes that following the Lord in faith has serious consequences, such as the suffering, persecution, and hardship he experiences in his apostolic ministry in Corinth (1 Cor 4:10-13). However, he feels compelled to preach the Gospel despite the personal cost (1 Cor 9:15). Reading the Corinthian text allows us to visualize some of the difficulties both Paul and the church face. Both persevere in their search for an authentic response to the Gospel and for the most effective use of their gifts in the service of others. This struggle characterizes Christian life in any transitional period, an experience with which we identify as a church in transition.

In this early period, various expressions describe the commitment of Christian believers; they are called "apostles," "disciples," and "missionaries" as well as being distinguished by their specific ministerial gifts. *Apostleship* is not a function of baptism but the result of a special call by God to perform a specific function. The Scriptures indicate that disciples of Jesus, such as Peter, are commissioned a second time after Jesus' resurrection (Mt 28:16-20; Lk 24:44-50; Acts 2:1-22). Not so for Paul, whose "apostleship does not build upon a prior discipleship" (Beker, *Apostle*, 5). Apostles are usually itinerant rather than residential preachers, with the source of their authority outside the community, as in the case of Paul (Petersen 123). Paul indicates that he understands the parameters of his role as an apostle in the

Corinthian church when he states: "We, however, will not boast beyond limits, but will keep within the field that God has assigned to us, to reach out even as far as you. For we were not overstepping our limits when we reached you; we were the first to come all the way to you with the good news of Christ" (2 Cor 10:13-14).

The term "disciple" is far more inclusive than "apostle" since it designates all followers of Christ. Missionaries could be apostles or disciples, and their work extends beyond individual communities of faith. Paul's coworkers include apostles such as Junia and Andronicus, missionaries such as Prisca and Aquila, and ministers who assume various leadership functions such as Phoebe. The Christians in Corinth form a community of disciples or saints, who assume diverse roles for the sake of the Gospel. While the call to follow the Lord is not as dramatic for all Christians as it was for Paul, ministry is part and parcel of life for all believers (1 Cor 12). Whatever the term we use to convey our Christian commitment, we, too, must be aware that ministry is integral to our call in faith. Throughout the course of our lives, our service will change, but Christian faith requires some concrete manifestation of belief on behalf of others.

Paul As an Apostle

For the Corinthian church, Paul becomes an example of an apostle in action, even though he calls himself the "least of the apostles" (1 Cor 9:1-2; 15:9-10). He assumes his apostolic responsibility in a variety of ways and speaks of his integrity as a preacher of the word. "For we are not peddlers of God's word like so many; but in Christ we speak as persons of sincerity, as persons sent from God and standing in his presence" (2 Cor 2:17). Paul writes the Corinthian church, visits them three times (1 Cor 4:18-19; 16:5), sends Timothy to Corinth in his place (1 Cor 4:17), teaches and admonishes the community (1 Cor 5:9.11; 6:18-19), and hands on the tradition to them (1 Cor 15:3). Likewise, Paul accepts affliction and suffering as part of ministry (2 Cor 1:5-8), works with the community (2 Cor 1:24), seeks mutual reconciliation (2 Cor 5:18-20), challenges the Corinthians to share their resources with other churches (2 Cor 8:14), and renews his dedication despite adversity (2 Cor 12:9-10). As an apostle, he encourages mutual service on the part of the community toward its missionaries, ministers, and leaders (1 Cor 16:15-16). In these descriptions, we can discover some of our own many ministerial responsibilities.

Paul's designation as an apostle is clear and consistent in 1 and 2 Corinthians. In Acts of Apostles, Luke limits the title "apostle" to the Twelve with only two exceptions involving Paul and Barnabas, demonstrating a more restricted usage in that later period (Kendall 301). Paul indicates to the Corinthian church that both he and Barnabas refuse some of the rights of apostles, namely, the right to hospitality, to marriage, and to community support (1 Cor 9:3-6). Indeed, Paul prides himself on his independence, continues his manual labor while he ministers in Corinth, and does not accept financial support from this church. In so doing, he opens himself to misunderstanding by the Corinthians, causing them humiliation rather than relieving them of a burden (Barrett, *2 Corinthians*, 281). "When the proclaimer receives remuneration, it is a sign of recognition for the preacher, but also an honor for the community" (Georgi, *Opponents*, 240). While in the case of the Corinthians Paul's financial independence may lead to further deterioration of his relationship with the community, the support of missionaries was a recognized custom in this early period. Emerging groups, like the Corinthian women prophets, hear Paul's refusal of support as "a rejection of friendship among equals" (Wire 195). Even today, Christian ministers carefully discern the acceptance of this custom of support, attempting to keep the proclamation of the Gospel in proper focus.

The Characteristics of a True Apostle

Most impressive in the Corinthian correspondence is Paul's analysis of an authentic Christian apostle or minister. In 2 Corinthians, he couches his positive statements in the rhetoric of boasting, forced to defend himself in light of misunderstanding and personal opposition by the Corinthian church. Paul knows that the Corinthians would describe a true apostle as one eloquent in speech and impressive in wisdom and theology (1 Cor 1-4). However, Paul counters their emphasis with a theology of the cross, and his "apostolic behavior is a reflection of his Christology" that focuses on power in weakness (Barrett, *2 Corinthians*, 49). Commitment to the Gospel enables Paul to embrace the hardships, abuse, loneliness, and conflicts of his ministry. From these experiences and his understanding of Christ, the apostle makes sense out his life and ministry. As we read the appropriate sections of these letters, Paul's words ring true because they bear the marks of the struggle that forged them into his memory.

Several sections of the letters to the Corinthians offer insight into Paul's understanding of apostleship and Christian ministry. The table on the next page locates the significant passages and offers a brief comment on the content of the sections.

TABLE 8: APOSTLESHIP AND MINISTRY IN THE CORINTHIAN LETTERS

1 Cor 1:17-4:21	Discussion of wisdom and folly; theology of the cross; role of apostles and leaders; contrasts between the Corinthians' view and Paul's understanding of his role as an apostle
1 Cor 3:21-4:13	Ridicule of the achievements of human leaders; hardship as proof of apostleship; paradox of Christian ministry
1 Cor 9:1-27	Rights of apostles; Paul's rejection of privileges; adaptation in ministry; openness to the outsider
1 Cor 12:1-31; 14:1-40	Gifts of ministry; working together in ministry; unity and diversity of the body of Christ; proper use of gifts in the churches
1 Cor 13:1-13	Love as the guiding principle and motivation in ministry
1 Cor 15:5-11	Post-resurrection call of apostles; grace of the call; ministry as a response
2 Cor 2:14-4:6	Qualities of the minister; aspects of ministry; proclamation and perseverance
2 Cor 4:1-12; 6:4-10	Paradoxes in ministry; qualities for effective ministry
2 Cor 3:7-4:6	Ministry of the new covenant
2 Cor 4:7-5:10	Ministry and mortality
2 Cor 5:11-21	Ministry of reconciliation
2 Cor 10:1-18	Paul's defense of his ministry
2 Cor 11:1-12:13	Paul's boasting of his apostleship, credentials, ministry, hardships, revelation, commitment; false apostles; qualities of ministry and of true apostles within the Fool's Speech
2 Cor 12:12	Signs of true apostle
2 Cor 13:3-4.10	Paradox of Paul's ministry in face of opposition; right use of apostolic authority

From the texts of 1 and 2 Corinthians, we have a fair idea of Paul's views of his own status as an apostle and his perspective on authentic Christian ministry. While most of the above selections in the correspondence have a harsh and combative tone, the contemporary reader can learn much from an assessment of the underlying qualities that Paul advocates for the true apostle and disciple of the Lord. Considering that Paul himself was a part-time, not full-time, missionary, his achievements in Corinth and the early church were certainly astounding (Banks 153). Paul's high standards and deep commitment, so evident in 1 and 2 Corinthians, challenge ministers today in whatever capacity they serve. Rather than cut off dialogue with this difficult church, Paul continues the conversation, although he conveys as attitude of frustration and disgust at their contrary views, particularly in 2 Corinthians 10-13. Within this context, one of his comments to the church seems an understatement: "And, besides other things, I am under daily pressure because of my anxiety for all the churches" (2 Cor 11:28). Another smacks of irony: "I think that I am not in the least inferior to these super-apostles" (2 Cor 11:5). However, Paul preaches, "For we do not proclaim ourselves; we proclaim Jesus Christ as Lord and ourselves as your slaves for Jesus' sake" (2 Cor 4:5), and this colors his approach to his life as an apostle and contributes to his view of ministry.

Qualities of Apostles and Disciples

Although Paul speaks extensively about his own apostleship in his letters to Corinth, he also questions the ministry of other apostles and missionaries in Corinth, as well as the community's own Christian commitment. Because the letters contain these multiple challenges, Christians today can reflect on the qualities Paul identifies as indicative of their own Christian response to God's call and examine their commitment against his criteria.

In his most heated discussion of his apostolic role, Paul parallels his credentials to those who oppose him. "Are they Hebrews? So am I. Are they Israelites? So am I. Are they descendants of Abraham? So am I. Are they ministers of

Christ? I am talking like a madman—I am a better one: with far greater labors, far more imprisonments, with countless floggings, and often near death" (2 Cor 11:22-23). Although his call is from God, Paul enumerates his sufferings, hardships, and experiences in great detail and with a sense of pride, leaving the community to assess the obvious contrasts to other Corinthian ministers. Boasting and foolishness characterize the last chapters of 2 Corinthians, but the recipients understand Paul's point against the opponents.

While Paul willingly acknowledges his earlier persecution of Christians (2 Cor 4:2), he now speaks with candor and pride of his Jewish background and heritage. Although the sufferings involved in his arduous travels coincide with his understanding of the place of the cross in Christian life, he demonstrates that trials and hardships characterize authentic life and ministry for the believer. Paul reminds us, as well as the Corinthian church, to respect our background as not only integral to our identity, but also as preparations for ministry. In addition, he suggests that we embrace the practical hardships and suffering associated with pastoral work as part of the ministry itself. Paul's approach and attitude turns negative experiences into positive opportunities—a realization stemming from his understanding of God's power and wisdom at work in Christ's death on the cross.

Paul also speaks about revelations and a thorn in his side in this major section (2 Cor 12:1-9). The extraordinary prayer experience certainly validates Paul's apostolic role in the Corinthians' eyes, since they desire these ecstatic gifts of the Spirit. However, the reference to the thorn puzzles commentators to this day. Is it a physical disability, such as a persistent pain in the head or ear, or an affection of the eye? Is it a mental challenge, such as depression? Is it a spiritual torment, such as temptation? Or is it the pain and persecution Paul experiences in his ministry, notably with this church? (Furnish 548-549). In light of the Corinthian correspondence, the trials of ministering in this community seem severe enough to warrant praying three times, typically understood as a prayer in distress. Perhaps, the sufferings in our own ministry are similar to those of Paul—the communities with which we expend the most time and energy are often the source of our deepest suffering. We can readily identify with Paul's prayer and, hopefully, with his extraordinary perseverance.

Positive qualities of Christian discipleship also come to the fore in these letters. For Paul, the apostle understands equality in Christ, has knowledge and humility, proclaims the Gospel as a service to the community, embodies the truth of Christ, and loves the community (2 Cor 11:5-11). Paul himself takes pride in the community, experiences joy and consolation from God and the church, and exhibits hope and courage (2 Cor 7:4-7; 3:12). Trustworthiness, forbearance, kindness, and truthful speech also mark the true apostolic leader (2 Cor 4:1-3; 6:4-8). "The signs of a true apostle were performed among you with utmost patience, signs and wonders and mighty works" (2 Cor 12:12). Paul's sufficiency is from God (2 Cor 3:5-6), and he does all for the sake of the Gospel (1 Cor 9:23). Whether in gentleness or strength (2 Cor 10:1), Paul embraces his responsibility for the church and, in doing so, invites us to do the same.

Effectiveness in Ministry

Reading the passages on ministry in 1 and 2 Corinthians enables us to identify the elements that account for the effective spread of the Gospel in the early church. Ministry, according to the gifts of the Spirit, embraces diversity, works toward unity, and is motivated by love (1 Cor 12-14). Believing in Christ and understanding our empowerment by the Spirit enables Christian ministers to have a proper perspective on their own roles in the service of others. Paul demonstrates sensitivity to outsiders in his own mission to the Gentiles and asks that the Corinthians be mindful of their witness to and concern for those outside their faith community (1 Cor 14:23-25; 2 Cor 9:1-15). In his long relationship with the church, Paul exhibits resilience, perseverance, and adaptability, qualities that allow for longevity in ministry (1 Cor 9:20-22). He is also willing to use various approaches in his service of the church, such as affirmation, challenge, exhortations, argument, and boasting, as these letters indicate. Furthermore, Paul has the ability to theologically assess both his success and his failure, seeing the wisdom and power of God always at work. Prayer, continued discernment, and collaboration with others constitute effectiveness for Paul. However, if the Corinthian correspondence reflects the true outcome of the apostle's relationship with the church, ending as it does with the harsh letter, then Paul's long-term effectiveness in this church is an open question. How difficult a result for someone like Paul to accept, and for us as well!

These qualities for effective ministerial involvement speak to us today, since our situations often parallel those of the early church. Appreciating diversity of gifts and utilizing them for the sake of the Gospel, without reference to gender, ordination, or legalistic approaches, present us with a real challenge since church structures often reflect other priorities. Working toward unity in a spirit of love and understanding opens us to new insights and possibilities, but this remains a long-term process. Paul's centering in Christ and recognition of the Spirit at work in the community enables him to empower others to take responsibility for their lives. A strong, solid, and authentic interpretation of the essence of the Gospel allows us to do the same.

Since Christians are often a minority group in our areas of ministry, sensitivity to those outside our faith community becomes essential. We live in a global community and our local church is a microcosm of that reality. Ministry that opens itself to broad needs will be effective in the long run; partnering with others in this endeavor insures benefit to all. Paul's example in these letters challenges each to us to be flexible, resilient, expansive, and persistent. We must reinvent ourselves, as did Paul in his long relationship with the Corinthian church, if we are to grow in and through our service to others.

We, like Paul and the Corinthians themselves, make mistakes, choose inappropriate language or methods, but we continue in ministry if our theological foundations and spirituality embrace these dimensions of life in healthy ways. Ministry today is a process, not a package; it calls for discernment of directions, not quick answers to questions; it pays attention to long-term effectiveness, not short-term success. Paul, in his letters to this church, embodies a gamut of qualities and emotions in his apostolic work. As we reflect on these manifestations of his frustration and his love, we cannot help but be touched by the reality of his situation. Perhaps, ours looks better by contrast!

A Perspective on Boasting and Imitation

Most of us find Paul's reliance on *boasting* an affront to our Christian sensibilities. He did as well! He frequently suggests no boasting (1 Cor 1:29; 3:21; 5:6; 9:16) or "boasting in the Lord" (1 Cor 1:31; 2 Cor 10:17). Recognition that all we have is gift from the Lord should diminish this approach (1 Cor 4:7). However, Paul himself uses this technique in appropriate and inappropriate ways (2 Cor 1:12.14; 7:4; 10:8-13; 11:30; 12:11). Paul boasts because his honor is at stake. Personal opposition calls for a strong response on his part, and so he assumes the technique used by his opponents. Within these boastful statements we discover Paul's views and those of ministers who follow "another Jesus" (2 Cor 11:4). By the strength of his expressions, he hopes to persuade the Corinthian Christians to a more favorable assessment of his Gospel proclamation and apostolic ministry.

Boasting generally produces powerful reactions in an audience. Indeed, underlying Paul's twenty-nine references to boasting in 2 Corinthians (fifty-five in the undisputed letters of Paul) is the brutality and harshness of human experience itself (Roetzel, "Dying," 10). But, the apostle utilizes this approach for a very specific purpose. In his boasting, Paul links himself with the suffering Christ and, for him, this is the heart of Christian understanding of apostleship and discipleship. We need to go beyond the arrogance in the text in order to understand Paul's intention. Our ministry of education and preaching calls us to convey the complexity of texts like these in ways that do not damage the self esteem of hearers of the word. Putting the text in its proper context helps in this regard.

Imitation elicits another powerful response in contemporary Christians. For Paul, Christians embody the values of Christ, and so they become models who actualize the presence of Christ in their unique life situations. Paul calls for others to imitate him because he imitates Christ; he is a mediator of the example of Christ (1 Cor 4:15-16; 11:1). When others see him, they should understand something of Christ and the Gospel. However, it is important for us to understand that Paul does not imply slavish imitation in his exhortation, nor does he value uniformity in our Christian response. Rather, Paul suggests that just as he interprets and discerns his responses to the Gospel, so must we. As educators and teachers of the word of Scripture, we must not only convey to our communities the power of example and the significance of role models, but also insure the unique response of individuals to the Lord's gifts. This approach calls for sensitivity to diversity and the ability to reinterpret the Gospel for new times, places, and situations.

Living Out the Call in the Corinthian Church

Paradoxes of Christian Life and Ministry

The gift of faith is a prerequisite for understanding one's call to discipleship, and only by faith does a person understand the paradoxes involved in living out that call. A paradox is something contradictory or contrary to our expectation. What a mystery for the Corinthians, and ourselves, to see life in death, joy in suffering, blessing in persecution (1 Cor 4:11-13; 2 Cor 4:8-10; 6:8-10). Only through an understanding of Christ crucified, do we even begin to touch the depths of this seemingly contradictory proclamation of faith. Paul's conviction regarding the transforming effects of Christ's death enables him to declare: "For I decided to know nothing among you except Jesus Christ, and him crucified" (1 Cor 2:2). In the cross, Paul sees not only the dimension of death but also the dimensions of resurrection, life, and exaltation (Beker, *Apostle*, 205). Both affect the way we live out our call as disciples of the Lord by directing our attention to new interpretations of suffering. Paul uses his own ministry as an example of these principles at work as he identifies true wisdom and power in the crucified Lord of glory (1 Cor 2:1-12).

The apostle to the Gentiles makes extensive use of paradox to engage the Corinthians in a practical application of theological insights to their own life and ministry. If a paradox "functions in the Pauline writings as a primary method of examining reality" (Fisher 222), then the Corinthian letters drive home a difficult message about Christian life and ministry. Paul describes his own experience. "We are afflicted in every way, but not crushed; perplexed, but not driven to despair; persecuted, but not forsaken; struck down, but not destroyed" (2 Cor 4:8-9). So convinced is he that Christian life is best understood by the contrast of opposites, that Paul makes seven paradoxical assertions in the short span of three verses (Fallon 56). "In honor and dishonor, in ill repute and good repute. We are treated as impostors, and yet are true; as unknown, and yet are well known; as dying, and see—we are alive; as punished, and yet not killed; as sorrowful, yet always rejoicing; as poor, yet making many rich; as having nothing, and yet possessing everything" (2 Cor 6:8-10). Only by faith can such a person be described as possessing all things (2 Cor 5:7), for Paul's message contradicts human wisdom, assessment, and understanding.

Some of the most difficult preaching and teaching we do in our ministry revolves around the harsh realities of life. While most of us eagerly affirm our faith at Sunday celebrations, many of us falter when put to the test in our daily struggles. Injustice in the workplace, conflict in relationships, lack of affirmation and false accusations from significant others, the climate of mediocrity within institutions, anxiety about health, family, job, and effectiveness, are but a few examples of the situations that sap our energy. Theoretical acceptance of the paradox of Christian life is not helpful in these moments. Modifying our attitudes and behavior to reflect our faith convictions is the challenge each one of us faces. Do we bring the perspective of faith to the daily challenges we encounter? How can we identify opportunities for growth in these difficult experiences? Where do we find life and hope as we struggle with hardship and adversity? How do we make sense out of sickness, suffering, and death, especially when these are unexpected and particularly tragic? Ministers who direct their attention to these questions discover the inadequacy of simple answers.

Paul gives us a reality check as he identifies the paradoxes of Christian life and ministry for the Corinthian church. But Paul does more than mere identification. He does not waver from his own commitment as an apostle in the face of adversity but allows his hope to sustain him. "So we do not lose heart. Even though our outer nature is wasting away, our inner nature is being renewed day by day" (2 Cor 4:16). As ministers and educators, we may not be as articulate as Paul in addressing the contemporary paradoxes of Christian existence. However, we can reflect on the biblical text and retell our personal stories of challenges to our faith. Our growth experiences may engage our communities in a significant reassessment of their own lives, just as Paul's accounts stimulated the Corinthians' thinking and discernment. The following paradoxes from the Corinthian letters might be a starting point for reflection and discussion within our families and communities as we deal with the contradictory values at the heart of Christianity.

Wisdom and Folly

Wisdom is a Corinthian topic, and Paul's understanding of wisdom mirrors the very different view of the Corinthian church (Conzelmann 57; Wire 61). According to Paul, the Corinthians adhere to the wisdom of this age along with the rulers of the world (1 Cor 2:6-8), a perspective contrary to the wisdom of God revealed through the Spirit (1 Cor 2:6-15). Those who are spiritual and mature apprehend God's wisdom, as opposed to the situation Paul finds among the Corinthians whom he calls "infants in Christ" who are "not ready for solid food" (1 Cor 3:1-3). Christian wisdom is "a knowledge of God's secret purpose" or God's plan for all humankind (Thrall 26). Paul sees the divine purpose unfolding in the crucified Christ he proclaims.

Paul speaks of wisdom (*sophia*) twenty-six times in the first four chapters of 1 Corinthians, and he states early in the letter that not many of the Corinthians are wise, powerful, or of noble birth at the time of their call (1 Cor 1:26). We often think of this particular passage as exclusively referring to the social status of the members of the Corinthian church. However, underlying this statement is a triad, the wise/powerful/rich, used by the prophet Jeremiah (Jer 9:22). The components of this triad are "not simply descriptions of social location, but are essential elements in a theological critique" (O'Day 264). Paul's purpose in his wisdom theology is a redefinition of God's saving action in Christ Jesus. The wisdom of the cross marks Christians from the rest of the world (Lampe 125). In the cross of Christ, God confounds human wisdom and makes this folly wisdom in God's sight. The Corinthian community can witness to this paradox by embracing the cross as Paul did. Jeremiah's word finds a new social context for interpretation in the Corinthian community (O'Day 266). We can also use it as a lens to theologically assess our own Christian experience and to discover anew the true meaning of wisdom and folly.

In his preaching of wisdom and foolishness to the Corinthians, Paul takes an unpopular position. He understands how the Corinthians will initially receive his words, but his understanding of the mystery of Christ leaves him no alternative but to preach the contradictory message of the Gospel. He draws out the implications of an "upside down" way of thinking, leaving the community little option but to rethink their approach to Christian life. For today's preachers of the Word, unpopular issues and themes surface in the Scripture readings as well as in church life. Our resolve to be faithful to God's Word must be as strong as Paul's. Our voice must be as prophetic as his, reinterpreting a difficult message in a new social and religious context. "For God's foolishness is wiser than human wisdom, and God's weakness is stronger than human strength" (1 Cor 1:25).

Power and Weakness

Paul uses another paradox to further expand his insight: "But he said to me, 'My grace is sufficient for you, for power is made perfect in weakness.' So, I will boast all the more gladly of my weaknesses, so that the power of Christ may dwell in me. Therefore I am content with weaknesses, insults, hardships, persecutions, and calamities for the sake of Christ; for whenever I am weak, then I am strong" (2 Cor 12:9-10). He speaks of the power of the cross (1 Cor 1:18),

Christ as the power of God (1 Cor 1:24), and God's weakness as stronger than human strength (1 Cor 1:25). Undoubtedly, Paul sees God's power at work in Christ and in the world. However, this power clothes itself in the weakness of humanity, and Paul urges the Corinthians to realize their true condition. He reminds the church that "God chose what is foolish in the world to shame the wise; God chose what is weak in the world to shame the strong; God chose what is low and despised in the world, things that are not, to reduce to nothing things that are" (1 Cor 1:27-28). The persecution Paul continually faces in preaching the Gospel to the Corinthian church is, for him, a concrete manifestation of weakness. However, he gains a perspective on this adversity when he reflects on Jesus. "For he was crucified in weakness, but lives by the power of God. For we are weak in him, but in dealing with you we will live with him by the power of God" (2 Cor 13:4).

Paul's way of understanding weakness as power is radically different from our contemporary perspective. We tend to shun weakness and the weak as ineffective, spineless, and unmotivated. However, Paul does not suggest that we assume a martyr complex, but rather that we understand our true human condition and the necessity of God's transforming power in Christ and in us. Reliance on the paradoxical wisdom of God leads to life, strength, and effectiveness because we open ourselves to divine power that works in mysterious ways. In Paul's mind, living according to this faith conviction should characterize Christian existence in the early church and today. The Corinthians found it difficult to accept and to live out this aspect of discipleship, and Paul, like ministers today, attempts to show the validity of this radical faith approach to life. He becomes a model for us in his embodiment of power in weakness in his own ministry (2 Cor 6:4-10; 12:10).

Shame and Honor

Paul interweaves unexpected interpretations into his understanding of Christian existence. He states: "We are fools for the sake of Christ, but you are wise in Christ. We are weak, but you are strong. You are held in honor, but we in disrepute" (1 Cor 4:10). The question of the Corinthians' honor smarts with irony from the apostle whose status was diminished by his conversion. In this period, honor was ascribed and acquired because of a socially recognized claim to worth, such as being male, Jewish, or a Roman citizen. In addition, honor could be achieved by excelling over others (Corrigan 24; Malina 47). Rather than clinging to his social dignity and worth, Paul embraces hardship and difficulties, often speaking in terms of servitude and shame. The Corinthians recognize honor in apostles and religious leaders by their letters of recommendation, ecstatic religious experiences, rhetorical skills, and extraordinary gifts—all of which Paul shuns. His criteria reflect God's perspective. "But God chose what is foolish in the world to shame the wise; God chose what is weak in the world to shame the strong" (1 Cor 1:27).

Paul again suggests a reversal of the world's values. While he does not discount using the Spirit's gifts and growing in faith, recognition of Christian values epitomized in the cross of Christ implies different standards and motivation. This teaching has a prophetic ring for the Corinthian church since it devalues their interpretation of the effects of Christ's death. While contemporary Christians hesitate to speak of honor and shame, achievement, recognition, rewards, economic and social status, and other visible signs of self-worth play an important role in our ecclesial and work life. The preacher has a delicate task in presenting Christian values, while challenging people to grow and develop. Perhaps, Paul's message suggests that honor, self-esteem, and personal worth come from within us and in our recognition of God's gift. External trappings or difficulties in ministry reveal little of the power of God at work—Christians see with the eyes of faith and often come to different conclusions.

Lessons for Christian Disciples

Living out their Christian call is a challenge for both Paul and the Corinthian church. While they understand mission and ministry as part of the call to apostleship and discipleship, the practical implications of faith in Christ crucified provide them with a daily challenge. Transformation in Christ occurred, but the reality of the cross challenges any worldly assessment of wisdom, power, and honor. Paul's theological critique of his own Gospel proclamation and ministry and his challenge to the church in Corinth provide us with points for consideration of our own ministerial situations.

As we reflect on our Christian call, do we include outreach in ministry as part of our commitment, as did the Corinthian Christians? Do we have a realistic view of ministry in the church today, appreciating the dual dimensions of suffering and transformation? What is our experience of the sacrifices and hardships of ministerial involvement? If Paul is an example to us of a suffering servant, how do we model what we preach in the moments that test our commitment? How does our life reflect the paradoxical values of the Gospel? How can we authentically preach weakness in a world that seeks power? Where do we see Christians contradicting the values of the world by their life choices, public statements, and social connections?

Paul reflected on the fuller meaning of Christ's death and reassessed his own effectiveness in ministry from the new paradigm of life in death. How do we describe the theological basis for our prophetic action and analysis? Paul challenged the Corinthians to on-going discernment (2 Cor 13:5). In what specific ways do we reassess our values, directions, faith, and ministry?

Paul presents us with a formidable task in these Corinthian letters, one that allows us to understand and integrate distinctive Christian values into our life and ministry. The message he presents sounds unfair, demanding, and contradictory at times. Even the messenger, Paul, is suspect by the Corinthian church. However, a prophetic voice has a ring of truth even when the words are "weighty and strong" (2 Cor 10:10).

Essential Aspects of Mission and Ministry in Corinth and Beyond

Mission in the Early Church

Exploring the Corinthian correspondence has been a journey with Paul and this church through the many facets of their growing and challenging faith relationship. What happened in Corinth, however, reflects something of the development of other Christian communities in New Testament times. Paul's letter to the Galatians and Matthew's Gospel address conflicts and difficulties in the development of the early church (H. Doohan, *Leadership*, chapter 2; L. Doohan, *Matthew*, chapter 2). However, most impressive to people of faith today is the spirit, vision, and energy of the early Christians. Their motivation is belief in the Gospel preached by Paul and other missionaries, and communities like Corinth are eager to hear the good news for it affected their lives in practical and wonderful ways.

Some of the difficult issues Paul faces in Corinth are the result of the enthusiasm with which the Corinthians embrace their faith in Jesus. They attempt to live out their interpretation of the Gospel within their own social, philosophical, religious, and urban environment, something Paul as a traveling apostle does in an entirely different way. The Corinthian Christians, like most of us, live out their faith response among people they know and within the predictable parameters of their daily life. On the other hand, Paul and his coworkers organize their mission, identify strategies, travel extensively, and usually deal with problematic issues from a distance. No wonder some of Paul's reflections are controversial and his advise scorned by the church in Corinth.

However, the Corinthians realize Paul's total commitment even though absent from their community, and they must admire his own openness to the radical message of the Gospel. Paul's tremendous energy in time spent, letters written, emissaries sent, reflection, teaching, and admonitions offered must impress the Corinthians, even though

153

they often disagree with the apostle's emphasis. Paul's sense of mission leads him to respond to the needs of communities as a pastoral theologian. His theology and missionary activity support, inform, and inspire each other. This dynamic theological development not only challenges Paul in his assessment of situations in the various communities but also provides practical insights for the church in Corinth, as the letters attest.

The mission of the early church is expansive, exciting, exploratory, and energetic. It generated enthusiasm just as an inspiring and challenging vision of church continues to motivate ecclesial communities today. Ministers and educators, sharing their convictions, theology, and practical suggestions, can pastorally create a vision of church that will expand our horizons and give the Gospel message a more contemporary flavor.

Paul's Focus on Ministry

A sense of mission leads to ministry in the Corinthian church, ministry according to the gift of the Spirit. The human dimensions of ministry emerge in the Corinthian letters, ministry characterized by joy, comfort, suffering, misunderstanding, and hope. Paul says to these Christians "But we have this treasure in clay jars, so that it may be made clear that this extraordinary power belongs to God and does not come from us" (2 Cor 4:7). How well does the image of earthen vessels describe all who minister in the church, whether in Corinth or in contemporary communities. Paul teaches us that whatever the outcome of ministry, "in the Lord your labor is not in vain" (1 Cor 15:58).

Ministry within the community of faith is as important as outreach in service. Insights into ministry emerge within the context of mutual involvement for Paul and the Corinthians, and we too will gain insight into our own ministerial challenges as we reflect on our experiences. Paul views ministry as a gift that develops within the human condition. In a letter such as 2 Corinthians we see not only the human dimensions of ministry but also the humanity of Paul in its weakness and strength. What hope the Scripture offers us in the apostle to the Gentiles!

The Corinthian letters offer a perspective for discerning ministerial effectiveness as well as Christian choices. Paul sees his own apostolic work in terms of building up the community of faith. "Now, even if I boast a little too much of our authority, which the Lord gave for building you up and not for tearing you down, I will not be ashamed of it" (2 Cor 10:8). He also views the utilization of the Spirit's gifts in a similar way. "On the other hand, those who prophesy speak to other people for their upbuilding and encouragement and consolation" (1 Cor 14:3). Effectiveness in ministry leads to personal and communal growth. In Corinth, this growth occurred within a diverse community that Paul consistently challenges to deeper unity and Christian love. He urges us to understand our role as ministers as well. "So with yourselves; since you are eager for spiritual gifts, strive to excel in them for building up the church" (1 Cor 14:12).

Collaboration and Partnership in the Corinthian Church

The Pauline mission is fundamentally a collaborative mission, and the Corinthian correspondence testifies to partnership among coworkers in the early church. Paul could not function as an apostle were it not for collaborative work on many levels of community life. Women and men assume responsibility for community development and mission; married couples like Prisca and Aquila, and celibates like Paul himself work in partnership to proclaim and spread the Gospel; households of faith like those of Stephanas and Chloe offer hospitality and places for gathering. The focal point is mission, not a specific missionary—a fact Paul emphasized in Corinth when factions develop among the followers of Paul and Apollos.

The Corinthian letters indicate that "from the very beginning Christian ministry was collaborative" (Harrington 63). Collaborative ministry emerges from Paul's understanding of church, from his conviction regarding the communal use of gifts, and from his commitment to foster unity, diversity, and mutuality. Coworkers are women and men, married and single, offering their service as apostles, ministers, missionaries, leaders, and deacons. While biblical translations sometimes foster the idea that certain roles were limited because of gender, the letters of Paul indicate otherwise, as we have noted. "Minister," "missionary," "apostle," "servant," "leader," and "deacon" apply to anyone gifted by the Spirit for that service. The Spirit's gifts are not gender specific in the early church; neither do community attitudes exclude women from specific ministry. Prisca, Aquila, Phoebe, Apollos, Timothy, Sosthenes, Chloe, and many others associated with Corinth whom we would call "laity" further the mission of the church by their travel, support, leadership, teaching, mentoring, and hospitality. All ministers, including Paul, considered themselves coworkers with God. "For we are God's servants, working together; you are God's field, God's building" (1 Cor 3:9).

These colleagues form a circle of personal and ministerial support for Paul and one another in a period of transition during which the church embraces the Gentile world, clarifies its identity in relation to Judaism, and reinterprets the message of Jesus. How supportive the Scripture is of our interests, efforts, and desires since Vatican II. Paul and the Corinthian church would affirm our efforts toward collaborative ministry, our inclusion of all the baptized in various forms of ministry, and our development of support systems to enhance personal growth and ministerial effectiveness. Our attempts at inculturation, ecumenical sensitivity, and biblical interpretation would also be applauded because the Corinthian letters witness to similar approaches. However, both Paul and the Corinthians would challenge discrimination in church leadership, gender discrimination in ministry, as well as our emphasis on structure, precedent, and legal codes to limit involvement in specific ministries. For the Corinthian church, and for ours, it is the best and the worst of times.

Paul's letters provide us with remarkable challenges as we minister in various capacities and with limited resources at this point in the history of our church. Just as Paul respected the tradition and developed it in light of new circumstances, so must we respect the tradition we have received from Scripture and from the church so that a truly new creation will emerge once again. The first-century disciples that come to life in 1 and 2 Corinthian offer example and hope to dedicated Christians today in their vision for Corinth and beyond. They saw great possibilities for the spread of the Gospel in their world; new places fascinated them; people's ideas and interchange enlivened them. The breadth and depth of their missionary interest affects our Christian vision as our world approaches the third millennium.

For Personal and Group Reflection

1. Discipleship and ministry went hand in hand in the early church. How do you demonstrate your following of the Lord Jesus in your service of others?

2. The apostle Paul identified qualities that the authentic minister of the Gospel should embody. What qualities do you believe are necessary for ministry in the church today?

3. The Corinthian letters witness to the effectiveness of ministry in the early church. What qualities did you see in Paul that contributed positively to his work?

4. The letters frequently contain statements that are difficult for contemporary readers to understand. How do you understand Paul's boasting and his challenge for imitation of himself? How effective can these approaches be in your ministry?

5. Paul saw many paradoxes in Christian life that he reflected on in his assessment of wisdom and folly, power and weakness, shame and honor. Which of these paradoxes describe you and your ministry in the church? In what ways?

6. As you reflect on Paul's understanding of discipleship and ministry, what lessons can

you apply to your own ministry in the church?

7. Paul viewed his ministry within the larger context of the mission of the church. How does your ministry contribute to the mission of the church today? What convictions regarding the church and its mission give you energy and hope?

8. Collaboration and partnership were evident in the Corinthian church as individuals used their gifts for building up the community of faith. What is the basis for collaboration today? What examples of working together do you see in your own ministry?

9. Collaboration requires faith in the presence of the Spirit, attitudes of respect, trust and love, and qualities that facilitate dialogue. How can you foster a more collaborative spirit by your ministry? What seems to hinder real partnership and collaboration in the contemporary church?

10. The Corinthian letters reflect a church eager for growth and struggling for identity. For Paul and the community, it was the best and worst of times. What parallels do you see in your experience of the church today? How and why do you continue to minister in these times of hope and despair?

Chapter Seven

Celebrating in New Times and Places

Exploring the meaning of Paul's letters to the Corinthian church has taken us on a journey to the first-century world of faith, commitment, inquiry, and interpretation. The Corinthian church accepted the Gospel preached by Paul with enthusiasm and developed their ideas in light of their own experience and situation. Paul's continuous dialogue with this community through visits, emissaries, and letters offers us a fresh and realistic picture of life in the early church. As we read through the Scripture readings in the various liturgical cycles, we should be mindful of the underlying struggles that gave rise to Paul's words. The context is often missing in the short liturgical selections, and so we give references to the fuller development of these passages in the book.

Liturgy is a celebration of life, and the energetic and enthusiastic life of the Corinthian church should be an inspiration for all Christians. The difficulties Paul encountered in the service of the Gospel are also a sign of hope to those of us who minister in churches that reflect the best and the worst of times, as did the church in Corinth. Paul continued in his ministry despite opposition, and grew in his understanding of the Gospel through his work with others. We are called to do the same and to minister according to the gifts we have received. Effectiveness for Paul, and for us, is the work of the Lord, and we know that the ways of the Lord are mysterious indeed!

Cycle A

CATECHETICAL FOCUSES FOR THE READINGS IN CYCLE A

Lord's Supper	1 Cor 11:23-26	Gathering around the table of the Lord
Easter Sunday	1 Cor 5:7b-8a	Celebrating the new covenant
2nd Sunday of the Year	1 Cor 1:1-3	Called by God
3rd Sunday of the Year	1 Cor 1:10-13. 17	Living the Gospel
4th Sunday of the Year	1 Cor 1:26-31	Understanding Gospel paradox
5th Sunday of the Year	1 Cor 2:1-5	Proclaiming the Word of the cross
6th Sunday of the Year	1 Cor 2:6-10	Proclaiming the wisdom of God
7th Sunday of the Year	1 Cor 3:16-23	Living as disciples of the Lord
8th Sunday of the Year	1 Cor 4:1-5	Ministering as the Lord's servants
Christ the King	1 Cor 15:20-26a.28	Handing over the kingdom of God
Trinity Sunday	2 Cor 13:11-13	Living in God
Corpus Christi	1 Cor 10:16-17	Sharing the body and blood of Christ

Lord's Supper (ABC): 1 Corinthians 11:23-26

Gathering around the Table of the Lord

The celebration of the Lord's Supper marks a profound event for the Christian community. In Paul's account the context of the words of institution of the Eucharist is a meal, celebrated within a household of faith. This assembly of Christians provides a realistic setting for the early church, and Paul challenges some of the practices of the Corinthian church in these gatherings. However, the meal itself reminds the early church of the Jewish Passover and the meal Jesus celebrated with his friends the night before he died. Many of the rituals of thanksgiving, blessing, sharing prayer, bread, and wine come from known religious customs of the day. However, in this earliest account of the Eucharist, Paul focuses on Jesus' actions and indicates that the sacrifice of Christ is *for us*. Bread broken and wine shared is done "in remembrance of me."

Paul hands on this tradition to the church in Corinth. This Christian community, gathered around the table of the Lord, is the body of Christ, and it must witness to the Lord's love by its unity and service to others. Today's church gathers, celebrates, remembers, serves, and during this special week, reminds all Christians of the central events of salvation in Christ.

Easter Sunday (ABC): 1 Corinthians 5:7b-8a

Celebrating the New Covenant

In this brief alternative reading for Easter, Paul focuses on the sacrifice of the Christ, the paschal lamb, and draws on Passover imagery to convey his message to the Corinthian church. Before the celebration of Passover, Jewish families, according to custom, rid their home of any old leaven so that they could begin anew the seven days of the festival that followed the Passover meal (Ex 12:15; 13:6-10). Such must be the case for the Christian community in Corinth. Paul challenges them to wipe out the old leaven of inappropriate behavior and values so that they might enter into the new covenant in Christ. The apostle links commitment and conduct for this community who, like ours, must walk in sincerity and truth. As we celebrate our faith in Jesus, the risen Lord, Paul asks us to live according to that belief in our daily lives.

Second Sunday of the Year (A): 1 Corinthians 1:1-3

Called by God

The readings for this time in the liturgical year come from the first four chapters of 1 Corinthians, which focus on factions, wisdom, power, and the cross. Since Paul will address issues, questions, and concerns throughout this letter, he begins with an introduction that reflects his call to apostleship and identifies the paradoxical message of the Gospel.

The Jewish Scriptures emphasize God's call of great figures, such as the prophets, in their history of salvation. Accordingly, the Christian church recognizes the call of Jesus when the Spirit descends upon him and he begins his ministry of salvation. Likewise, Paul acknowledges his own call by God to be an apostle to the Gentiles in these introductory verses of 1 Corinthians. With this recognition of his special vocation, Paul conveys to the community the authenticity of the Gospel he preaches and the direction of his mission. The apostle addresses the Christians in Corinth as saints and as a church sanctified in Christ Jesus, and offers them greetings of grace and peace.

While the introduction to 1 Corinthians is typical of Paul's letters, recognition of God's gift and call is a key element for Paul and all Christians. Sensitivity to religious experience, understanding our mission, and courage to live according to the Gospel are challenges Paul offers to the Corinthians, and to us, in the remainder of this letter.

Third Sunday of the Year (A): 1 Corinthians 1:10-13.17

Living According to the Gospel

Paul begins to draw out the implications of the Corinthians' call to discipleship. Recognition of the problem of divisions and factions in Corinth causes distress to the apostle, since unity in Christ is the Gospel message. The Corinthian church sets one religious leader against another, often valuing external qualities such as eloquence and wisdom above the difficult message of the cross of Christ. Paul's intent is to preach the Gospel and, in the following sections of 1 Corinthians, he begins to draw out the implications of the death of Christ for the church. Responding to the call of the Lord affects the individual and the community, and so Paul appeals for unity, harmony, and appropriate values. The kinds of divisions experienced by Christians in Corinth still affect our church today, but our commitment challenges us to address difficult situations so that we may witness to our unity and purpose in Christ.

Fourth Sunday of the Year (A): 1 Corinthians 1:26-31

Understanding the Gospel Paradox

These last verses of the chapter identify the paradoxical values of the Gospel that contradict human wisdom and understanding. Paul indicates something of the background of the Corinthian church when he speaks about their situation at the time of their call. They represented a cross-section of society, but God works through them because of the life they share in Christ. However, Paul offers this church a deeper challenge than acceptance of diversity. He suggests a new theological perspective to confront their way of thinking and acting. Because of his understanding of the death of Christ, he focuses on weakness rather than power; foolishness instead of wisdom; shame in place of honor. While Paul's insight emerges from his reflection on God's action in Christ, the Corinthian church thinks no differently than their society. Their willingness to live according to these Gospel values would be a real test of commitment.

Understanding the radical and paradoxical message in this reading continues to challenge Christians today, and we, like the Corinthians, often prefer a more acceptable interpretation than the one Paul offers.

Fifth Sunday of the Year (A): 1 Corinthians 2:1-5

Proclaiming the Word of the Cross

Paul continues to develop his paradoxical interpretation of the Gospel relating the elements of God's wisdom and power to his own ministry in the Corinthian church. He downplays human wisdom, lofty speech, and a formidable approach in dealing with the church, in favor of God's wisdom and power of the Spirit. As an apostle, Paul understands that his effectiveness is at stake in this community. He continues, in this letter, to present knowledge of Christ Jesus as the true wisdom of God. God's action in and through the death of Jesus turns human criteria upside down. Since Paul ministers according to these Gospel standards, he challenges the Corinthian church, so fascinated with eloquence in the proclamation of the mystery of God, to accept his humanly unappealing message and ministry. His preaching will never meet their expectations if they continue in their understanding of Jesus.

Underlying the letters to the Corinthian church is Paul's appeal to the community to reassess their interpretation of the Gospel against his. In so doing, they will not only grow in faith, but they will also present a more authentic Christian witness. Believers today must accept the same challenge as the Corinthians to continually reassess their understanding of the scriptural message.

Sixth Sunday of the Year (A): 1 Corinthians 2:6-10

Proclaiming the Wisdom of God

Paul continues to use contrast in his comparison of the wisdom of God and the wisdom of this age. God's wisdom is hidden, secret, and revealed to us through the Spirit. More than knowledge, this understanding comes through divine insight, and so it requires an openness to God's revelation. By contrast, human and worldly wisdom misses the reality perceived by faith, namely, that Jesus is the crucified Lord of glory. Glory was an expression used of God in the Jewish Scriptures, but Paul uses it for Jesus, thus associating the splendor of Yahweh with Christ. As the apostle continues to develop his ideas of wisdom, he challenges the Corinthian Christians to spiritual maturity since these ideas require new openness to the revelation of the Spirit.

While knowledge or enlightened faith is important for Christians in Corinth ánd now, Paul places his emphasis on truths that require God's movement in our hearts and minds. These mysteries of faith are the ones that constitute the heart of the Christian experience and surpass any prior revelation to humankind. Understanding God's wisdom requires openness to the Spirit and reflection on the mysteries of faith, challenges Paul offers to believers today if we are to proclaim the deeper meaning of the Gospel.

Seventh Sunday of the Year (A): 1 Corinthians 3:16-23

Living As Disciples of Christ

In an earlier section of this letter, Paul asks where is the wise person, the scribe, and the ruler of this world, questioning whether God makes foolish the wisdom of this world (1 Cor 1:20). Now he brackets his intervening response with a statement that the wisdom of this world is foolishness with God (1 Cor 3:19), a recurring theme throughout the entire section. Underlying Paul's lengthy discussion is an attempt to persuade the Corinthian church to embrace a new level of faith and to live according to the Gospel he preaches. For the sake of his argument, Paul shifts his focus to his understanding of church. The Christian community is God's temple because it is empowered by the Spirit of God. This reality leads to a reversal of the values of the world, and therefore, whether Paul speaks about wisdom, folly, human leaders, or apostolic preachers, new criteria should determine the Corinthians' assessment of their worth.

Paul's challenge to live according to the confounding message of the Gospel rings true in our own contemporary situations when we often experience a blurring of boundaries between worldly and Christian values. We, like the Corinthians, must remember our identity in Christ so that we will translate the Gospel into our approach to life.

Eighth Sunday of the Year (A): 1 Corinthians 4:1-5

Ministering As Servants of the Lord

Paul begins this chapter with a description of his role, using servant of Christ and steward of God's mysteries. In his use of servant, the apostle indicates his dependence on the Lord and his relationship to the community. Paul is keenly aware that he, like all Christians, receives the gift of faith and the call to proclaim the Gospel. However, referring to his apostolic task on behalf of the Corinthian church, Paul sees himself as a steward of the mysteries of God. He has a special relationship to this church as its founder, and he feels a unique responsibility to insure its growth in their Christian response. Since the Corinthians question his credibility, Paul specifies trustworthiness in relation to his stewardship role as an apostle. He further confounds their assessment of his ministry by placing any judgment of himself or others to God, whose commendation will rest on their inner motivation.

Difficulties surround Paul's proclamation of the Gospel to the church in Corinth. However, he, like ourselves, must continue to rely on the Lord and act according to the vision we have received. As servants of the Lord, the effectiveness of our ministry will only come to light when we receive our commendations from the Lord.

Thirty-Fourth or Last Sunday of the Year (A)
Christ the King: 1 Corinthians 15:20-26a.28

Handing Over the Kingdom to God

This selection identifies the risen Christ as the new Adam and contains a Christian apocalypse (vs 23-28) that Paul utilizes to focus on Christ's role in the parousia. Paul begins with a statement on Christ's resurrection and immediately links it to the resurrection of Christians. Through contrasts that associate death with Adam and life with Christ, Paul vividly portrays the effects of each of these representative figures on humankind. With the sin of Adam, the human condition changed, and death became part of humanity's fate. In the risen Lord, humanity experiences transformation and the promise of its own resurrection. However, Paul points to parousia in this passage when he sees the destruction of death itself and the subjection of all things to Christ (Ps 8:6; 110:1). In the end, Christ will hand over everything to God and will, himself, be subject to God.

While we understand the religious usage of the reign or the kingdom of God in the Scriptures, the idea of king or kingdom resonates little with those who live in democratic societies. However, we do understand power, influence, victory, death, destruction, and life, language Paul uses to impress the Corinthian church with the final outcome of God's action in Christ. The power of God over all things indicates our total dependence on God and the proper order of the universe. Sin and death no longer have power over those of us redeemed in Christ. A new order prevails; a new hope is ours; we will be part of the final victory of Christ and God. This celebration allows us to focus on the end, so that we may reintroduce the values of Christ more fully into our daily lives.

Solemnity of the Lord:
Sunday after Pentecost, Trinity Sunday (A):
2 Corinthians 13:11-13

Living in God

Paul ends the Corinthian correspondence with final greetings to the members of the church, appealing to them to live in harmony and peace. The great theme of unity within the body of Christ is a message they heard from Paul many times. The letters also document the many disagreements between Paul and the Corinthian church, and so this call for agreement, love, and unity suits the situation of the church very well. Most remarkable is the unique theological statement in the last verse that speaks of the grace of the Lord Jesus Christ, the love of God, and the communion of the Holy Spirit. We recognize the trinitarian language in this blessing. Paul uses it to refer to the life, love, and union that we share as believers. God's action through Christ gives us life and grace, and the Spirit continues to work in us so that the love of God will be fully manifest in our lives.

However, we describe our own experience of God, we must reflect the biblical insight of our union with the Lord and one another in love. The attributes of God are the very ones that Paul urges the Corinthian church to develop. If we understand the grace, love, and union we share in God, then we will reflect these qualities in our lives.

Solemnity of the Lord:
Thursday after Trinity Sunday, Corpus Christi (A):
1 Corinthians 10:16-17

Sharing the Body and Blood of Christ

Paul speaks about the Lord's Supper in this passage and in 1 Corinthians 11:23-26. In both instances the context for the celebration is a meal with ritual actions. Taking the cup, offering a blessing, breaking and sharing bread would be familiar actions to Jews and Greeks, and so Paul reminds the Corinthian church of these aspects of the celebration. However, the context for this remembrance gives rise to practical concerns for Paul and the Corinthian church. Consequently, in this chapter Paul addresses the question of eating food offered to idols, and in chapter 11 the abuses within the Christian assembly. The sharing of the body and blood of the Lord is a celebration of the community, and unless the community reflects unity and love, the celebration becomes empty ritual.

Remembering the words, actions, and sacrifice of the Lord is the focus of today's celebration. Living as the one body of Christ is the purpose of our Christian life. In Paul's mind, there is an intimate connection between worship and life. The integration of our eucharistic celebrations with the witness of our lives is the challenge offered to the Corinthian church and to us as well.

Cycle B

CATECHETICAL FOCUSES FOR THE READINGS IN CYCLE B

1st Sunday of Advent	1 Cor 1:3-9	Awaiting the day of the Lord
3rd Sunday of Lent	1 Cor 1:22-25	Proclaiming the foolishness of the cross
Lord's Supper	1 Cor 11:23-26	Gathering around the table of the Lord
Easter Sunday	1 Cor 5:7b-8a	Celebrating the new covenant
3rd Sunday of the Year	1 Cor 7:29-31	Responding with a sense of urgency
4th Sunday of the Year	1 Cor 7:32-35	Pleasing the Lord
5th Sunday of the Year	1 Cor 9:16-19.22-23	Ministering in the Lord's name
6th Sunday of the Year	1 Cor 10:31-11:1	Imitating Christ
7th Sunday of the Year	2 Cor 1:18-22	Witnessing to the fidelity of God
8th Sunday of the Year	2 Cor 3:1b-6	Living as a new community
9th Sunday of the Year	2 Cor 4:6-11	Persevering in Christian ministry
10th Sunday of the Year	2 Cor 4:13-5:1	Hope in times of difficulty
11th Sunday of the Year	2 Cor 5:6-10	Growing in faith
12th Sunday of the Year	2 Cor 5:14-17	Seeing in new ways
13th Sunday of the Year	2 Cor 8:7.9.13-15	Responding generously to need
14th Sunday of the Year	2 Cor 12:7-10	Experiencing God's power in weakness

First Sunday of Advent (B): 1 Corinthians 1:3-9

Awaiting the Day of the Lord

Paul begins all his letters, with the exception of Galatians, with thanksgiving for God's wonderful action in Christ and for the community's response in faith. As part of their new life in Christ, the Corinthian church experienced the presence of Spirit's gifts, such as speech and knowledge, an indication to them of the richness of their life as believers. While they seemed to enjoy many spiritual gifts in their community, Paul challenges the Corinthians to put greater emphasis on their waiting and hoping for the day of the Lord. The fullness of God's revelation in Jesus is still ahead of us, and Paul indicates that the Corinthian Christians will be strengthened until that final day comes.

Advent is our special time of waiting for new manifestations of the Lord and for the fullness of life. Unlike the Corinthians who felt God's promises were already fully realized in their lives, we watch, wait, and hope for the day of the Lord. While we appreciate the Lord's gifts in our lives, we continue to proclaim the good news and grow in our understanding of the place of Jesus in God's design. Until we participate in fullness of life that is our expectation, we can rely on God's fidelity and our partnership in Jesus, the Lord, to be ready for that day.

Third Sunday of Lent (B): 1 Corinthians 1:22-25

Proclaiming the Foolishness of the Cross

In the early chapters of 1 Corinthians, Paul proclaims the folly of the cross and draws out the implications of his theological perspective for Christian life and ministry. The founder of the Corinthian church initiates a discussion of power and wisdom because these Christians relied on the world's standards, rather than God's, and they assessed Paul's teaching in light of these false values. To proclaim the crucified Christ as the power and wisdom of God was a startling contradiction for both Jews and Gentiles. However, Paul understands the paradoxes of Christian life and so identifies strength in weakness, life in death, wisdom in folly.

This way of thinking reflects the paradoxical teaching of Jesus in the Gospel and indicates the difficult path for Christians as they continually strive to live in ways that contradict society's values.

Paul knows that his radical interpretation of the cross will be difficult for the Corinthian church to hear and to understand. However, he offers a prophetic word that still challenges today's Christians who must live according to standards that contradict human assessments of power, wisdom, and strength.

Lord's Supper (ABC): 1 Corinthians 11:23-26

Gathering around the Table of the Lord

See the commentary in Cycle A.

Easter Sunday (ABC): 1 Corinthians 5:7b-8a

Celebrating the New Covenant

See commentary in Cycle A.

Second Sunday of the Year (B):
1 Corinthians 6:13c-15a.17-20

Following the Lord

Within a section on abuses, lawsuits, and ethical issues in the Corinthian church, Paul speaks of the connection between the future resurrection of Christians and present immorality within the community. He confronts Corinthian attitudes that denigrate the physical body and deny the moral consequences of their present behavior by drawing out the implications of their union with Christ. The value of the human person emerges in this section because of the way Paul deals with difficult moral issues. The apostle identifies the Christian's union with Lord, the community's identity as the body of Christ, and the resurrection of Jesus as the basis for hope in our own resurrection. Furthermore, he informs the church that union with the Lord means that they share the Spirit and that their bodies house that God-given Spirit.

Paul reminds the Corinthians of these profound understandings of church in this section in order to draw out some practical consequences for Christian life. Faith convictions should affect personal choices and patterns of behavior. Our actions, like those of the Corinthians, have implications not only for the present, but also for the future.

Third Sunday of the Year (B): 1 Corinthian 7:29-31

Responding with a Sense of Urgency

These few verses indicate Paul's understanding of the short time that remains before the second coming of the Lord. In fact, the entire chapter, with its views of marriage and celibacy, must be understood from this eschatological perspective. Paul and the Corinthians expected the end within their lifetime (1 Cor 15:51). Therefore, Paul urges that things of the world, marriage, mourning, and rejoicing be seen from the vantage point of the end. While Paul understands that we become holy in our situation in life (1 Cor 7:24), he identifies a focus that will enable the Corinthians to live according to the Lord's call.

Reflection on the end times is useful for Christians today, since it allows us to assess our choices in light of our final destiny. This perspective and Paul's sense of urgency challenge the Corinthians, and ourselves, to respond immediately and totally to God's call. It also allows us to appreciate the transitoriness of this world so that we can identify the true center of our Christian commitment.

Fourth Sunday (B): 1 Corinthians 7:32-35

Pleasing the Lord

This reading addresses the anxieties all Christians experience, anxieties that Paul wants the Corinthians to put in perspective. Primary for the Corinthians' consideration is how to focus on things of the Lord in light of the impending end. Paul's choice of the example of married couples being anxious about their partners and affairs of the world probably startles many in the Corinthian church. How could Paul say such a thing in light of the work of missionary couples, the commitment of the households of faith, and the ministry of so many responsible Christians? However, a firm commitment to the Lord in light of the nearness of the end is the overriding concern of Paul in this letter. This perspective is important for contemporary Christians to understand, otherwise the passage becomes even more oppressive than it sounds.

The challenge of Paul to insure a proper attitude and orientation in our lives is a lesson for the early church and ourselves. While Paul has a personal preference for celibacy, he acknowledges that different lifestyles reflect God's gift to each one within the community (1 Cor 7:7). The point is for all Christians to give priority to their relationship with the Lord with an inner freedom of mind and spirit.

Fifth Sunday of the Year (B):
1 Corinthians 9:16-19.22-23

Ministering in the Lord's Name

In this entire chapter, Paul speaks about his apostleship and defends his decisions, particularly to minister without payment from the Corinthian church. These verses indicate Paul's commitment to the Gospel and convey his sense of obligation to live out his call to service by proclaiming the Gospel. Interestingly, the apostle speaks of his adaptability to various groups so that all might share in the blessings of Jesus' message. A key characteristic of Paul's ministry is his ability to accommodate to different situations and circumstances. While his opponents might label him inconsistent, the apostle demonstrates a quality needed by ministers today as we work in diverse cultural, religious, and social settings.

Proclamation of the Gospel includes interpretation and adaptation to new times and peoples. In addition, just as Paul expected misunderstandings of his ministry, so too must we be prepared to renew our commitment despite the difficulties we encounter.

Sixth Sunday of the Year (B): 1 Corinthians 10:31-11:1

Imitating Christ

After speaking of his own role as an apostle and challenging the community in terms of its morality and Christian witness, Paul calls for imitation of himself. Paul believes that the Corinthians know and understand Jesus because of what they see in their religious leaders and one another. Since Christians affect others by their lives and through their ministry, they must be authentic models of Gospel values so that their witness will contribute to the faith development of others. In addition, Paul indicates the power and value of Christian life when he suggests that we do everything for the glory of God.

Only when Christians today model Christ in their daily lives and ministry, do they provide the authentic witness to Gospel values that the world needs. Whether we minister in the church, provide leadership in the community, deal with issues in work or family, or respond to community needs, our attitudes and commitment will speak as clearly as our words and actions. Our integrity as Christians is the most valuable witness we offer.

Seventh Sunday of the Year (B): 2 Corinthians 1:18-22

Witnessing to the Fidelity of God

Paul begins this letter of reconciliation with words about his own ministry and a canceled visit to the church. In this section, he addresses issues regarding his ministry from a theological perspective, centering on the fidelity of God embodied in Christ. This point of departure for describing and defending his own ministry enables Paul to establish his own faithfulness to the Gospel and to speak of God's role in his work. Just as God is faithful, so is the apostle who proclaims the Son of God, Jesus Christ. This description of Jesus, unusual for Paul in his letters, indicates the special relationship between Jesus and the Father. The apostle also refers to his own unique affiliation with the community, and uses the baptismal imagery of anointing and sealing as a sign of Spirit to remind the church of his unique call, and theirs.

God inaugurates a new age in Christ, but Paul's ministry, as well as ours, reflects the fidelity of God. Likewise, God is at work in Paul, Silvanus, and Timothy as they preach the Gospel message with consistency and purpose. As we consider our own service in the church, we contemplate the reality of God's fidelity to us, our faithfulness to God's Word, consistency in sharing the message, and appreciation of the true source of our effectiveness in ministry.

Eighth Sunday of the Year (B): 2 Corinthians 3:1b-6

Living As a New Community

Paul continues to focus on ministry, identifying the fruits of his endeavors and drawing comparisons between himself and his opponents in Corinth. Since Paul founded this church, he does not need letters of recommendation as do other missionaries. The church itself, living according to the Gospel, is the greatest commendation for any apostle. Paul uses the language of the new covenant in this section, with its emphasis on the spirit of the Law, written within human hearts. The Gospel he preaches reveals this new relationship with God in Christ, and this message is life-giving for those who live accordingly.

Paul's ministry, as ours, reflects the newness, spirit, and life of the Gospel. Its effectiveness is visible in the community's response in faith. However, the role of the minister is secondary to the action of God that draws the community into a new level of relationship and commitment to the Lord. While Paul will later defend aspects of his ministry, he sets the stage for a faith assessment of his work by the Corinthian church.

Ninth Sunday of the Year (B): 2 Corinthians 4:6-11

Persevering in Christian Ministry

The focal point and model of ministry is Christ himself, and Paul begins this section with reference to light and glory of God reflected in the face of Christ. However, life for us comes through the death of Jesus, so Paul realizes that the vulnerability of the Christian minister is an opportunity to recognize the power of God at work. Paul uses images of the treasure in an earthen jar and speaks of affliction, persecution, and suffering in vivid terms when describing his work on behalf of the church. However, these difficulties do not crush Paul or drive him to despair. Rather, confidence and hope underlie his comments in order to illustrate for the church that effectiveness in ministry often comes from weakness.

This difficult lesson for the Corinthians, and ourselves, acknowledges that growth in ministry is primarily the work of God. Christians who understand the paradox of the Gospel message know that difficulties and effectiveness often go hand in hand in ministry and in life. Persevering in our commitment, despite difficulties, is a quality of ministry needed in today's church. However, Paul challenges us to recognize that God's power contributes more to our continued effectiveness than any of our gifts.

Tenth Sunday of the Year (B): 2 Corinthians 4:13-5:1

Hope in Times of Difficulty

Paul's use of the contrasting images of death and life, wasting away and renewal of spirit, earthly tent and eternal dwelling remind believers of their hope in new life. External realities often hide the inner transformation that Christians perceive in faith. Although future resurrection was far from the minds of the Corinthians who experienced the power of the risen Lord within their assemblies, the apostle identifies the connection between the resurrection of Jesus and their own future transformation. Christians, because of their faith, see something more than present life and look deeper than the obvious signs of decay around them. They celebrate life as they suffer affliction.

This faith perspective, along with hope in the resurrection, provides the basis for a true judgment of our present existence and ministry. Paul's insight that we are in the process of continual transformation and renewal guides his assessment of his own apostolic work, particularly when he has to deal with the harsh realities of the Corinthian church. For ourselves as well, faith and hope should mark our lives as a Christian people so that we will see hardships as stepping stones to glory.

Eleventh Sunday of the Year (B): 2 Corinthians 5:6-10

Growing in Faith

Paul speaks about a faith approach to life that makes him confident in the Gospel he preaches and in his understanding of ministry. In his use of the image of being at home or away from the Lord, Paul emphasizes the movement between present realities and future reward, rather than expressing a yearning for the end. The apostle has a profound conviction that Christian life is being in Christ. Believers can draw on the abiding presence and power of the Lord in every circumstance of life, and, therefore, human limitations do not impede the work of God. The apostle examines his own situation with the eyes of faith and expresses confidence in the Lord's work.

Paul links faith and commitment in this passage, noting that being at home with the Lord depends on the quality of our Christian life. However, because of the Corinthians' strong emphasis on the present, he also reminds them that what they do in the body will be judged and rewarded by the Lord. As Christians today, we too must walk by faith, grow in confidence, and continue in our commitment to the Christ. Paul suggests that our lives will continue to have meaning if we aim to please the Lord and live according to the Gospel.

Twelfth Sunday of the Year (B): 2 Corinthians 5:14-17

Seeing in New Ways

Paul continues to comment on his apostolic service by emphasizing the radical transformation brought about by Christ's death and its implications for the Corinthian church. No longer can believers live according to old standards, for now we are a new creation in Christ. Our faith allows us to appraise Christ and Christian life from a different point of view. Human judgments have no validity if we understand God's action in the death of Christ. Furthermore, the love of Christ, who died for all, motivates ministers and communities to continue in faith and hope.

Paul understands the implications of our identity as a new creation in Christ, and so he urges the Corinthian church to reassess their understanding of the Gospel and his apostleship. Christian transformation allows Christians today to view Christ and one another in new ways. Paul's words can inspire all believers to rethink their values, judgments, and perspectives in light of their union with Christ.

Thirteenth Sunday of the Year (B):
2 Corinthians 8:7.9.13-15

Responding Generously to Need

In chapters 8 and 9, Paul speaks about the collection for the poor in Jerusalem with these verses focusing on his appeal to the Corinthian church. He begins by commending their faith and spiritual gifts, but his affirmation is more about the Lord's work than their choices, since Paul has difficulty with the Corinthians' emphasis on gifts of speech and knowledge. However, the collection is important not only because of the presence of needy persons in the Jerusalem church, but also because the contributions of the Pauline communities are a sign of unity between the Jewish and Gentile churches. To indicate the collection's priority, Paul sends Titus to Corinth, notes the generosity of the Macedonian churches (2 Cor 8:6.16-19.23; 9:2-4), and identifies several reasons for the community's generous response. Paul reminds the community of the generous act of Jesus, who though rich became poor, indicating that the sinless one gave himself in death that we might live (2 Cor 5:21). The Corinthian church must imitate the Lord and do what is appropriate in their own situation.

However, Paul expands his theological reason for generosity by referring to balance, equality, and sharing of resources in the churches. He presents enough information for the Corinthians to choose their response, which he hopes will be an unselfish one. Paul recommends to the Corinthians a concrete manifestation of love and responsibility in their generous support of the needy. He not only challenges them to respond but reminds us as Christians to generously share our gifts.

Fourteenth Sunday of the Year (B): 2 Corinthians 12:7-10

Experiencing God's Power in Our Weakness

Paul's final letter to the Corinthians (2 Cor 10-13) contains difficult material, written in a harsh tone, that indicates the human response of the apostle in the face of continuous opposition and misunderstanding of his ministry. In the "Fool's Speech" (2 Cor 11:1-12:13) Paul identifies his credentials, defends his apostleship, undermines his opponents, and boasts about his ministry. Prior to this section, he speaks about his visions and revelations that would appeal to the Corinthian church who love extraordinary manifestations of the Spirit. Paul then indicates the thorn in the flesh given to him. Commentators through the centuries tried to identify this thorn, seeing it as anxiety, sexual temptation, physical illness such as a chronic eye ailment or headache, mental depression, rejection, or hardships in ministry. Physical illness is a possibility since sickness and demons were associated in this period, and Paul speaks about a messenger of Satan. However, thorns can also mean enemies (Num 33:55; Ezek 28:24), and Paul describes his rivals in terms of Satan in an earlier section (2 Cor 11:14). If we remember the opposition Paul encountered in the Corinthian church, this latter interpretation is just as feasible as some form of physical infirmity.

However, Paul uses this section to return to a favorite theme—that God's power is made perfect in weakness. For Paul, as for Christians today, embracing hardships, difficulties, and conflicts in ministry is a daily challenge. Only our faith understanding will allow us to see weakness, humiliation, and powerlessness as the opportunity for the Lord to work in and through us.

Celebrating in New Times and Places

Cycle C

CATECHETICAL FOCUSES FOR THE READINGS IN CYCLE C

3rd Sunday of Lent	1 Cor 10:1-6.10-11	Warnings against overconfidence
4th Sunday of Lent	2 Cor 5:17-21	Inviting others to be reconciled
Lord's Supper	1 Cor 11:23-26	Gathering around the table of the Lord
Easter Sunday	1 Cor 5:7b-8a	Celebrating the new covenant
2nd Sunday of the Year	1 Cor 12:4-11	Appreciating the diversity of spiritual gifts
3rd Sunday of the Year	1 Cor 12:12-30	Living as the one body of Christ
4th Sunday of the Year	1 Cor 12:31-13:13	The guiding principle of love
5th Sunday of the Year	1 Cor 15:1-11	Experiencing the risen Lord
6th Sunday of the Year	1 Cor 15:12.16-20	Believing in the resurrection
7th Sunday of the Year	1 Cor 15:45-49	Becoming a new person in Christ
8th Sunday of the Year	1 Cor 15:54-58	The culminating victory of God
Corpus Christi	1 Cor 11:23-26	See commentary for Lord's Supper

Third Sunday of Lent (C): 1 Corinthians 10:1-6.10-11

Warnings against Overconfidence

As part of his discussion on food offered to idols (1 Cor 8 and 10), Paul offers instruction from the Jewish Scriptures to the Corinthian church, recalling images of Moses, the sea, cloud, manna, and water from the powerful exodus experience. The cloud and sea are symbols for the Spirit and water of baptism; the manna and water from the rock point to the spiritual food and drink of the Eucharist. Connecting salvation history with the Christian tradition allows Paul to offer lessons to those in Corinth who experience the new call of the Lord. Paul reminds the church that although the Jewish community experienced the guidance of the Lord, Yahweh was not pleased with them because of their complacency and overconfidence.

The Corinthian community can learn from the history of its ancestors in faith and examine its own sense of security regarding conscience questions (1 Cor 8:12). While the church experiences a new freedom in Christ, it must guard against smugness and security in its choices and develop sensitivity to the conscience decisions of others. A warning similar to that given to the Israelites and the Corinthians holds true for Christians today. While the Lord's blessings and gifts abound, we cannot assume we please the Lord or that the fullness of salvation is ours. Our collective history indicates that we can misuse our freedom in Christ, and take for granted the guidance and care of the Lord. Paul challenges all Christians to remember their past and to watch lest they fall.

Fourth Sunday of Lent (C): 2 Corinthians 5:17-21

Inviting Others to Be Reconciled

Paul speaks extensively about his ministry in this letter to the Corinthian church. Recognizing his difficulties with the community make him aware of the profound need for their mutual reconciliation. He therefore recalls the theological foundation for his movement towards reconciliation with the church, namely, that we are a new creation, now reconciled to God in Christ. Christians experience transformation in their new relationship with God because God has reconciled the world. While Paul understands that this salvific action of God transforms humanity from its old existence to a new covenantal relationship, he urges Christians to respond to its higher demands. In this sense reconciliation is not only a gift we acknowledge but a process that requires our efforts.

The need for reconciliation continues in our present church and world, even though we accept God's transformational gift. To be reconciled is to experience salvation, peace, and love, signs of the new covenant in Christ. Paul's challenge to the Corinthian church to active involvement in the ministry of reconciliation is one that we also can take to heart. Perhaps the most significant lesson for us is that Paul takes the initiative in restoring a right relationship between himself and the church. His example is a powerful one for each of us when conflicts emerge in ministry, work, community, or family situations.

Lord's Supper (ABC): 1 Corinthians 11:23-26

Gathering around the Table of the Lord

See the commentary in Cycle A.

Easter Sunday (ABC): 1 Corinthians 5:7b-8a

Celebrating the New Covenant

See commentary in Cycle A.

Second Sunday of the Year (C): 1 Corinthians 12:4-11

Appreciating the Diversity of Spiritual Gifts

In response to a question from the Corinthian church (1 Cor 12:1), Paul offers reflections over three chapters (12-14), which we can describe as the foundations for collaborative ministry. He speaks of the variety of the Spirit's gifts, the unity and diversity of the body of Christ, the qualities of Christian love, and the use of the Spirit's gifts within the church. In this selection, Paul emphasizes that the same

Spirit, Lord, and God offer the varieties of gifts, services, and activities so visible in the Corinthian church. Because Christians share the same Spirit, they can work together for the good of all without competition. Gifts may differ, as they do, but the Spirit gives freely to each one. Paul reminds the community of this reality because of their misunderstanding of spiritual gifts.

Paul uses "variety" three times to emphasize the great diversity of the Spirit's manifestation in charisms, ministries, and activities within the church. Because each one has a different gift the community will only benefit when everyone works together. This incomplete list of gifts does not indicate priorities, as Paul does later in the chapter (1 Cor 12:28). However, by beginning with wisdom, knowledge, and faith Paul shows his awareness of the Corinthian's interest in these gifts. The apostle leaves the gift of tongues, a favored one in Corinth, to the end, and calls for interpretation of tongues. He also connects prophecy and discernment, recognizing the necessity of collaboration for understanding the meaning of these gifts in the faith community.

Christians today share a variety of gifts, given for the benefit of all in the community. The realization that we share the same Spirit and all receive these gifts from the Lord should foster a new level of partnership in ministry.

Third Sunday of the Year (C): 1 Corinthians 12:12-30 (longer) or 12:12-14.27 (shorter)

Living As the One Body of Christ

Following his identification of the gifts of the Spirit, Paul chooses the metaphor of the body, a living organism, to describe the Christian community. Paul reminds the Corinthians that they were all baptized into one body in the one Spirit. Baptism integrates social and religious distinctions into Christ, so that equality exists among members of the body. However, equality does not eliminate real diversity within the faith community. Diversity in the human body insures the proper working of all its life functions; so too with the body of Christ. Paul bases his counsel toward collaborative efforts in the Corinthian community on this understanding of church.

Many lessons emerge in this familiar biblical passage for the Corinthian church, subject as it was to factions and divisions, and for us, dealing with world values that compete with the Christian Gospel. Paul focuses on cooperation among members of the body by appreciating the gifts of others, understanding our interdependence, and working together with love, honor, and respect. The sufferings and joys of others affect each one of us, and so a sense of mutual responsibility emerges as we reflect on the reading. The Christian message challenges us to appreciate our communal ties and to witness to the presence of Christ as church.

The house churches in Corinth provided an environment where believers, whether they were slave, free, Jew, or Gentile, could work and celebrate together as equal partners. Apostles, prophets, and teachers proclaimed the Gospel, challenged and guided the community. And while Paul downplays the spectacular gifts extolled by the Corinthian church, he consistently seeks to create a new spirit of working together within the body of Christ. Our communities should provide similar atmosphere so that the diversity of gifts can be utilized for the good of whole church.

Fourth Sunday of the Year (C):
1 Corinthians 12:31-13:13 (longer) or 13:4-13 (shorter)

The Guiding Principle of Love

This beautiful selection on love contains very real challenges for the Corinthian church and ours. Living as the body of Christ, with the experience of the wonderful gifts of the Spirit, provides a daily challenge for the Corinthians. A guiding principle emerges here and throughout Paul's letters, that of Christian love. Paul uses the phrase "if I" in the opening section of the passage (vs 1-3) and enumerates gifts, such as tongues, knowledge, faith, prophecy, and almsgiving, showing their futility without love. The Corinthians were familiar with the images of bronze gongs and cymbals that Paul uses, and so his message is clear. The next verses speak about the qualities of love (vs 4-7), attitudes lacking in the

Corinthian church and attributes needed by the apostle as well. In the final verses (8-13) Paul returns to the gifts of the earlier section. Prophecy, tongues, and knowledge will cease because they offer partial views of reality. Only love will prevail in the end.

In this reading Paul identifies love as the one essential characteristic for all believers and suggests that love should guide every action, decision, and dimension of Christian life. Lest the Corinthians misunderstand the meaning of love, Paul offers concrete examples for their assessment. Christians today can identify these attributes and use them to measure the sincerity of their efforts in collaboration. Likewise, these attributes can be applied to any work, family, or community situation to assess the quality of its Christian life.

Fifth Sunday of the Year (C):
1 Corinthians 15:1-11 (longer) or 15:3-8.11 (shorter)

Experiencing the Risen Lord

In 1 Corinthians 15, Paul speaks about the resurrection of Christ, its consequences, the resurrection of our bodies, and final transformation. In this opening section, Paul reminds the community of his preaching and handing on of a tradition they accepted in faith. The death and resurrection, as a fulfillment of the Scriptures, is the central point of this creedal formula. Paul then speaks of the appearances of the risen Lord to Cephas, the Twelve, five hundred brothers and sisters, James, all the apostles, and, last of all, himself. Interestingly, Paul makes no distinction between his experience of the risen Lord and that of the other witnesses; it is the same Jesus. Paul's call to be an apostle and his preaching of the Gospel stem from this profound religious event.

This passage is significant for the Corinthian church in that it identifies the central proclamation of Christian faith. However, while Paul hands on a tradition to this church, he also identifies belief in the resurrection with an experience of Jesus who died, was buried, and now lives. The testimony of witnesses confirms the resurrection of Christ. For Christians today, the resurrection is central to our faith. We rely on the testimony of others, the credibility of Scripture, and teachings of the church for our affirmation of belief. However, the reading suggests that the disciples' experience of the risen Lord impelled them to proclaim the Gospel. Is our own faith based not only on the traditions handed down to us, but also on a personal experience of the Lord? Do we see Christian life and ministry as a response to our faith?

Sixth Sunday of the Year (C): 1 Corinthians 15:12.16-20

Believing in the Resurrection

Paul spends a significant amount of time on the question of the resurrection of Christ because of its connection to the resurrection of believers, a difficult teaching for the Corinthians. This church, so affected by the Greek mentality, gives primacy to the soul over the body and tends to minimize the importance of the body. Paul, on the other hand, views the human person as a unified whole and emphasizes the importance of the body. In a logical argument, the apostle shows how denial of resurrection from the dead has very specific consequences for the Corinthians' faith. Assuming the connection between Christ and each Christian, Paul states that if Christ has not been raised, his preaching is in vain, the Corinthians' faith is meaningless, and those who died are lost. Since the Corinthians affirm their experience of the risen Lord through the power of the Spirit, they cannot agree with the initial statement, and so their thesis falls.

Paul's understanding of the intimate connection between Christ and Christians comes from his conversion experience. He uses that insight in this reading and consistently draws out its implications in his letters. For Christians' today, this reading may contain unfamiliar logic, but we can identify with its faith conviction. Belief in Christ's resurrection is the source of hope in our final resurrection from the dead. This radical Gospel message calls for a comparable response in our preaching, ministry, and Christian life.

Seventh Sunday of the Year (C): 1 Corinthians 15:45-49

Becoming a New Person in Christ

Paul uses Adam and Christ in this selection to compare our present and future life. Drawing on Genesis 2:7, which states God made Adam a "living being," Paul extends the image to the last Adam, Christ, who becomes a "life-giving spirit" for us. In his comparisons between Adam and Christ, he speaks of physical and spiritual realities, earth and heaven, a person of dust and a person of heaven. While these contrasts are significant, this section only makes sense in light of what precedes it. In verses 35-44, Paul responds to questions regarding resurrection from the dead by using the image of sowing. When we bury a seed, a change takes place, and a plant emerges. While we realize the radical change that occurs, we also recognize the connection between seed and plant. Similar transformation takes place in the resurrection of the dead, and this is the hope of Christians.

The lessons for us revolve around the continuity that Paul stresses between this life and the next, as well as the radical change we anticipate. Paul challenges us, as he did the Corinthians, to live in light of the end since future glory depends on the quality of our Christian life. However, Paul also encourages hope in our future and complete transformation into Christ.

Eighth Sunday of the Year (C): 1 Corinthians 15:54-58

The Culminating Victory of God

In this final section of the chapter on resurrection, Paul speaks about God's ultimate victory and our full transformation in Christ. He uses apocalyptic language (1 Cor 15:52) in the preceding section to indicate the anticipated final coming of the Lord in glory, and here relies on vivid contrasts to complete the picture. Paul reminds the Corinthians that, in the end, our perishable and mortal bodies will be imperishable and immortal, and death will lose its sting. For this final victory over sin and death, Paul offers thanks to God, recognizing, too, that this wonderful action comes about through Christ.

After his culminating statement, Paul urges the Corinthians to be steadfast and immovable in their faith and to excel in the Lord's work. Paul's admonitions offer us a challenge to persevere and grow in faith, to continue to hope in our own resurrection from the dead, and to continue our Christian ministry. If we understand Paul's message we will think differently about life and death, and this will be our witness to the world.

Solemnity of the Lord:
Thursday after Trinity Sunday, Corpus Christi (C):
1 Corinthians 11:23-26

Gathering around the Table of the Lord

See Lord's Supper (ABC).

Celebrating together as a faith community is the central event for Christians. In these liturgical acts we remember our identity, our tradition, our heritage, and our life. The word of Scripture, so integral to these celebrations, becomes bread and life for us when we uncover the essence of its meaning. Adapting, reinterpreting, and proclaiming the Gospel message is the task of ministers and religious educators, just as it was for Paul and the coworkers. How we translate the Scriptures for new times and places depends on our knowledge, insight, study, and prayer. How we challenge our communities depends on our integrity, commitment, and spirituality. Paul and the Corinthian Christians provide us with materials, models, and challenges. We must do the same for one another.

Afterword

Ministering in the Best and Worst of Times

The Corinthian correspondence reveals an engaging portrayal of the early church, its leaders and ministers, its issues and interests. It was the best and the worst of times for Paul and the Christian community as they attempted to live the Gospel and to grow in their faith. Within the chapters and verses of these letters, we see Paul exercising leadership as an apostle in rapidly changing circumstances. His situation, and that of the Corinthian community, often mirrors our own ministerial challenges and opportunities. The parallels between Paul's time and ours, his ministerial leadership and ours, emerge in the pages of this book as we reflect on the meaning of the biblical text.

Paul ministers in an enthusiastic community that reflects the religious diversity and social differences of the Greco-Roman world. In order to effectively minister in Corinth and beyond it, Paul engages others in the spread of the Gospel. These factors and relationships affect Paul's exercise of leadership by insuring adaptation and innovation, facilitation and empowerment.

In the Corinthian correspondence we witness the deterioration of the relationship between Paul and the community. Ministering in the early church takes on a realistic and human perspective, and we can readily identify with these difficult circumstances that challenge Paul's leadership effectiveness.

In order to provide a solid foundation for Christian growth, Paul proclaims the Gospel, offers the fruits of his theological reflection to the community, and conveys in his letters valuable insights into the early church's understanding of God's work in Jesus and the presence of the Spirit. Christian leadership implies a vision of faith as the starting point for ministry.

However, Paul readily moves from a theological understanding of the Gospel to the practical issues of concern in the Corinthian church. He provides guidelines and principles for the community to discern its direction and identify the implications of belief for Christian life. His own ministerial leadership allows him to strongly present his own convictions and to challenge the community to seek Christian solutions to daily difficulties.

The spirit and the problems of the early church emerge in the celebrations of the Corinthian church. The realistic framework of worship, the need for reconciliation, and the hope of transformation provide insight into the areas of Paul's ministry and his leadership opportunities. He responds with direction, appeals, and insight. The community often offers its prayer to God in the midst of difficult and trying circumstances, a situation that reflects our ministerial joys and dilemmas.

Paul offers insight into the commitment of early apostles, disciples, and ministers in the Corinthian community. He personally experiences the dying and rising of Christ in his work with this community, giving a ring of truth to his own assessment of Christian ministry. Only faith transforms adversity into an opportunity for growth, and Paul's faith and perseverance offer hope to those of us who continue to experience the paradoxes of Christian life and ministry.

The liturgical readings from 1 and 2 Corinthians often need a context for understanding and interpretation. The Corinthian issues may not be ours, but the Corinthian's desire for growth and Paul's ministry on behalf of the church certainly can inspire and challenge those of us who minister in the best and worst of times.

As I rediscovered Paul in the research and writing of this book, I was personally challenged by Paul's perspective in this difficult ministerial situation. The conflicts, struggles, adversities, misunderstandings, and daily challenges often mirrored my own experiences and those of my colleagues in ministry. However, the passion, energy, and commitment of Paul, the coworkers, and the church enabled me to gain perspective and to renew my faith and hope. Ministering in the best and worst of times is the challenge we face, as did Paul and the Corinthian Christians.

Resources

Abbott, Walter, ed. *The Documents of Vatican II*. New York: Guild P, 1966.

Banks, Robert. *Paul's Idea of Community: The Early House Churches in the Historical Setting*. Grand Rapids: Wm. B. Eerdmans, 1980.

Barrett, C. K. *The First Epistle to the Corinthians*. 2nd ed. London: Adam and Charles Black, 1971.

———. *The Second Epistle to the Corinthians*. London: Charles Black, 1973.

Beker, Christian J. *Heirs of Paul: Paul's Legacy in the New Testament and in the Church Today*. Philadelphia: Fortress, 1991.

———. *Paul the Apostle*. Philadelphia: Fortress, 1980.

———. "Paul the Theologian: Major Motifs in Pauline Theology." *Interpretation* 43 (1989): 352-65.

Betz, Hans Dieter. *2 Corinthians 8 and 9: A Commentary on Two Administrative Letters of the Apostle Paul*. Philadelphia: Fortress, 1985.

Bornkamm, Gunther. *Paul*. New York: Harper and Row Publishers, 1969.

Bossman, David. "Images of God in the Letters of Paul." *Biblical Theology Bulletin* 18 (1988): 67-76.

Branick, Vincent. *The House Church in the Writings of Paul*. Wilmington, Delaware: Michael Glazier Inc., 1989.

Carlson, Richard P. "The Role of Baptism in Paul's Thought." *Interpretation* 97 (1993): 255-66.
Conzelmann, Hans. *1 Corinthians*. Philadelphia: Fortress, 1975.
Corrigan, Gregory. "Paul's Shame for the Gospel." *Biblical Theology Bulletin* 16 (1986): 23-27.
Crosby, MIchael H. *House of Disciples: Church, Economics, and Justice in Matthew*. New York: Orbis Press, 1988.
D'Angelo, Mary Rose. "Women Partners in the New Testament." *Journal of Feminist Studies in Religion* 6 (1990): 66-86.
Doohan, Helen. *Leadership in Paul*. Wilmington, Delaware: Michael Glazier Inc., 1984.
———. *Paul's Vision of Church*. Wilmington, Delaware: Michael Glazier Inc., 1989.
Doohan, Helen and Leonard. *Prayer in the New Testament*. Collegeville, Minnesota: Liturgical Press, 1992.
Doohan, Leonard. *Acts of Apostles: Building Faith Communities*. San Jose: Resource Publications, 1994.
———. *Laity's Mission in the Local Church: Setting a New Direction*. San Francisco: Harper and Row, 1986.
———. *Luke: The Perennial Spirituality*. Santa Fe: Bear and Co., 1985. (Distributed by Resource Publications, Inc., San Jose, California.)
———. *Matthew: Spirituality for the 80s and 90s*. Santa Fe: Bear and Co., 1985. (Distributed by Resource Publications, Inc., San Jose, California.)
Ellis, E. Earle. "Paul and His Co-Workers." *New Testament Studies* 17 (1970-71): 437-52.
———. *Prophecy and Hermeneutic in Early Christianity*. Grand Rapids: Wm. B. Eerdmans, 1978.
———. "Soma in First Corinthians." *Interpretation* 44 (1990): 132-44.
Fallon, Francis T. *2 Corinthians*. Wilmington, Delaware: Michael Glazier, 1980.
Fee, Gordon D. *The First Epistle to the Corinthians*. Grand Rapids: Wm. B. Eerdmans Publishing Co., 1987.
Filson, Floyd. "The Significance of the Early House Churches." *Journal of Biblical Literature* 58 (1939): 105-12.

Fisher, James A. "Pauline Literary Forms and Thought Patterns." *Catholic Biblical Quarterly* 39 (1977): 209-223.
Fiorenza, Elisabeth Schussler. *Bread not Stone.* Boston: Beacon, 1984.
———. *In Memory of Her.* New York: Crossroad, 1983.
———. "Rhetorical Situation and Historical Reconstruction in 1 Corinthians." *New Testament Studies* 33 (1987): 386-403.
Fitzmeyer, Joseph A. *According to Paul: Studies in the Theology of the Apostle.* New York: Paulist, 1993.
———. *Pauline Theology: A Brief Sketch.* New Jersey: Prentice Hall, 1977.
Forbes, C. "Comparison: Self Praise and Irony: Paul's Boasting and The Conventions of Hellenistic Rhetoric." *New Testament Studies* 32 (1986): 1-30.
Furnish, Victor P. *II Corinthians.* Garden City, New York: Doubleday, 1984.
———. "Belonging to Christ: A Paradigm for Ethics in First Corinthians." *Interpretation* 44 (1990): 145-47.
Gager, J. *Kingdom and Community: The Social World of Early Christianity.* Englewood, New Jersey: Prentice Hall, 1975.
Gale, Herbert Morrison. *The Use of Analogy in the Letters of Paul.* Philadelphia: Westminster, 1964.
Georgi, Dieter. *The Opponents of Paul in Second Corinthians.* Philadelphia: Fortress, 1986.
———. *Theocracy in Paul's Practice and Theology.* Minneapolis: Fortress, 1991.
Gillman, Florence. *Women Who Knew Paul.* Collegeville, Minnesota: Liturgical, 1992.
Hahn, Ferdinand. "Charisms and Office." *Theology Digest* 29 (1981): 239-243.
Hanson, A. T. *Studies in Paul's Technique and Theology.* Grand Rapids: Wm. B. Eerdmans Publishing Co., 1974.
Harrington, Daniel. "Paul and Collaborative Ministry." *New Theology Review* 3 (1990): 62-71.
Holmberg, Bengt. *Paul and Power: The Structure of Authority in the Primitive Church As Reflected in the Pauline Epistles.* Philadelphia: Fortress, 1980.

Hooker, Morna D. "Authority on Her Head: An Examination of 1 Cor XI:10." *New Testament Studies* 10 (1963-4): 410-16.
———. "Beyond the Things That Are Written? St. Paul's Use of Scripture." *New Testament Studies* 27 (1981): 295-309.
———. *Preface to Paul.* New York: Oxford, 1980.
Horsley, Richard A. "Consciousness and Freedom Among the Corinthians: 1 Corinthians 8-10." *Catholic Biblical Quarterly* 40 (1978): 574-89.
Hurd, J. C. *The Origin of First Corinthians.* London: SPCK, 1965.
Jeffers, James S. *Conflict at Rome: Social Order and Hierarchy in Early Christianity.* Minneapolis: Augsburg/Fortress, 1991.
Kee, Howard Clark. *Understanding the New Testament.* Englewood Cliffs, New Jersey: Prentice Hall, Inc., 1993.
Kendall, Daniel, and Gerald O'Collins. "The Uniqueness of the Easter Appearances." *Catholic Biblical Quarterly* 54 (1992): 307.
Kim, Seyoon. *The Origin of Paul's Gospel.* Grand Rapids: Wm. B. Eerdmans Publishing Co., 1981.
Lampe, Peter. "Theological Wisdom and the 'Word About the Cross': The Rhetorical Scheme in 1 Corinthians 1-4." *Interpretation* 44 (1990): 117-31.
LaVerdiere, Eugene. *Invitation to the New Testament.* Garden City, New York: Image, 1980.
Lohfink, Gerhard. *Jesus and Community: The Social Dimension of Christian Faith.* Philadelphia: Fortress, 1984.
Love, Stuart. "Women's Roles in Certain Second Testament Passages: A Macro Sociological View." *Biblical Theology Bulletin* 17 (1987): 50-59.
Maccoby, Hyam. *Paul and Hellenism.* Valley Forge, Pennsylvania: Trinity Press International, 1991.
MacDonald, Dennis Ronald. *The Legend and the Apostle.* Philadelphia: Westminster, 1983.
Malina, Bruce. *The New Testament World: Insights from Cultural Anthropology.* Atlanta: John Knox, 1981.
Martin, Ralph P. "The Spirit in 2 Corinthians in light of the 'fellowship of the Holy Spirit' in 2 Corinthians 13:14." In *Eschatology and the New Testament*, edited by W. Hulitt Gloer, 113-28. Peabody, Massachusetts: Hendrickson Publishing, 1988.

Mearns, C. L. "Early Eschatological Development in Paul: The Evidence of I and II Thess." *New Testament Studies* 27 (1980-81): 137-57.

Meeks, Wayne A. *The First Urban Christians: The Social World of the Apostle Paul.* New Haven: Yale, 1983.

Meyers, Eric M., and Michael L. White. "Jews and Christians in a Roman World." *Archaeology* 42 (1989): 27-33.

Munro, Winsome. "Women, Text, and Canon: The Strange Case of 1 Corinthians 14." *Biblical Theology Bulletin* 18 (1988): 26-31.

Murphy-O'Connor, Jerome. *1 Corinthians.* Wilmington: Michael Glazier, 1979.

―――. "Another Jesus (2 Cor 11:4)." *Revue Biblique* 97 (1990): 238-51.

―――. "Co-Authorship in the Corinthian Correspondence." *Revue Biblique* 100-104 (1993): 562-79.

―――. "The Corinth That Saint Paul Saw." *Biblical Archeologist* (Sept 1984): 147-59.

―――. "Eucharist and Community in First Corinthians." *Worship* 50 (1976): 370-85.

―――. *St. Paul's Corinth: Text and Archeology.* Wilmington, Delaware: Michael Glazier, 1983.

―――. *The Theology of the Second Letter to the Corinthians.* New York: Cambridge UP, 1991.

Nardoni, Enrique. "The Concept of Charism in Paul." *Catholic Biblical Quarterly* 55 (1993): 69.

O'Day, Gail R. "Jeremiah 9:22-23 and 1 Corinthians 1:26-31: A Study of Intertextuality." *Journal of Biblical Literature* 109 (1990): 259-67.

O'Meara, Thomas Franklin. *Theology of Ministry.* New York: Paulist, 1983.

Papahatzis, Nicos. *Ancient Corinth.* Athens: Ekdotike Athenon SA., 1978.

Patte, Daniel. *Paul's Faith and the Power of the Gospels.* Philadelphia: Fortress, 1988.

Petersen, Norman R. *Rediscovering Paul: Philemon and the Sociology of Paul's Narrative World.* Philadelphia: Fortress, 1985.

Plevnik, Joseph. "The Center of Pauline Theology." *Catholic Biblical Quarterly* 51 (1989): 461-578.

Reid, Barbara. "Problematic Paul on Women." *New Theology Review* 5 (1992): 40-51.

Richardson, P. "Pauline Inconsistency." *New Testament Studies* 26 (1980): 347-362.

Ridderbos, Herman. *Paul: An Outline of His Theology.* Grand Rapids: Wm. B. Eerdmans, 1975.

Roetzel, Calvin J. "As Dying and Behold We Live." *Interpretation* 96 (1992): 5-18.

———. *The Letters of Paul: Conversations in Context.* Atlanta: John Knox Press, 1982.

Sampley, J. Paul. *Walking Between the Times: Paul's Moral Reasoning.* Minneapolis: Fortress, 1991.

Schmithals, Walter. *The Office of Apostle in the Early Church.* New York: Abingdon, 1969.

Stanley, David M. "Idealism and Realism in Paul." *Way* 21 (1981): 34-46.

Stendahl, Krister. *Paul Among Jews and Gentiles and Other Essays.* Philadelphia: Fortress, 1976.

Swain, Lionel. *The People of the Resurrection: The Apostolic Letters.* Wilmington, Delaware: Michael Glazier Inc., 1986.

Theissen, Gerd. *The Social Setting of Pauline Christianity: Essays on Corinth.* Philadelphia: Fortress, 1982.

Thrall, Margaret E. *The First and Second Letters of Paul to the Corinthians.* Cambridge: UP, 1965.

Verner, David C. *The Household of God: The Social World of the Pastoral Epistles.* Chico, California: Scholars, 1983.

Wedderburn, A. J. M. "Paul and Jesus: Similarity and Continuity." *New Testament Studies* 34 (1988): 161-82.

Welborn, L. L. "On Discord in Corinth: 1 Corinthians 1-4 and Ancient Politics." *Journal of Biblical Literature* 106 (1987): 85-111.

Wire, Antoinette Clark. *The Corinthian Women Prophets: A Reconstruction Through Paul's Rhetoric.* Minneapolis: Fortress, 1990.

Ziesler, John. *Pauline Christianity.* New York: Oxford UP, 1983.

Index of Scripture References

Genesis
1:27-28 116
2:7 187
5:1-2 116

Exodus
12:14 121
12:15 161
13:6-10 161
24:3-8 121

Numbers
33:55 179

Deuteronomy
12:11-12 121
18:1-4 121

Psalms
8:6 167
110:1 167

Isaiah
52:1-7 64
55:11 121
6:1-13 136
6:8 74

Jeremiah
1:1-5 136
1:7 74
9:22 149
31:31 121

Ezekiel
2:3 74
24:5-8 121
28:24 179
41:22 121
44:16 121

Malachi
1:7-12 121

Matthew
26:26-29 120
28:16-20 136

Mark
14:22-25 120

Luke
22:15-20 120
24:44-50 136

John
4:53 86

Acts of Apostles
2:1-22 136
2:45 107
2:46 86
4:34-35 107
5:42 86
8:1.3 3
9:1-2.4-5.13-14 3
9:5 5
9:11 3
10:2 86

Index of Scripture References

Acts of Apostles (continued)
13-21.27-28 3
15:22 32
15:22-35 32
16:1-3 31
16:15 .... 85, 86
18:1-2 31
18:1-3 21
18:2 85
18:2.18.26 31
18:11-17 21
18:17-18 30
18:18-19 21
18:19.26 31
18:24-19:1 21
18:25-26 31
18:3 3
18:4-8 21
18:7 31
18:8 .... 85, 86
19:21 21
19:22 32
20:2 21
21:39 3
22:3 3
22:7-8 3
22:25-29 3
23:6 3
23:24-26 21
23:27 3
24:27 21
25:1 21
26:5 3

Romans
5:3-6 117
6:2-4 25
12:1-2 112
16 .... 32, 134
16:1 14
16:3 31
16:3.5 85
16:7.12.15 32
16:22 .... 7, 32
16:23 .... 30, 31, 32, 85

1 Corinthians
1-4 138
1-7 53
1:1 30
1:1-2 135
1:1-3 .... 39, 162
1:1.14.16 111
1:1-17 115
1:2 .... 112, 134
1:2.9 74
1:3 72
1:3-4 .... 1, 74
1:3-9 170
1:4-7 127
1:7 98
1:9 .... 72, 74
1:10 95
1:10.26 112
1:10-13.17 162
1:10-6:20 41
1:11 .... 22, 30, 39, 85
1:11-12 45
1:12 .... 28, 30, 45, 52
1:13 117
1:14 .... 21, 85
1:14.16 30
1:14-16 115
1:14-3:4 51
1:16 .... 85, 86
1:17 .... 65, 66
1:17.21.23 135
1:17-21 46
1:17-26 27
1:17-2:16 75
1:18 .... 73, 149
1:18-25 75
1:20 165
1:20-22 26
1:21 73
1:22-25 170
1:23 66
1:23-24 28
1:23-25 51
1:24 .... 73, 150
1:25 .... 149, 150
1:26 .... 19, 87, 107, 148
1:26-31 163
1:27 151
1:27-28 150
1:29 .... 106, 145
1:30 .... 72, 74
1:31 145
2:1 .... 73, 112
2:1-2 66
2:1-3 21
2:1-5 164
2:1-12 147
2:1-16 65
2:2 146

200

Index of Scripture References

2:2.8	74	4:20	73
2:4	135	5-6	101
2:5	72	5-12	94
2:6-8	148	5:1	101
2:6-10	164	5:1.11	28
2:6-15	148	5:1-13	101
2:7	73	5:2.6	101
2:8	76	5:4	74, 113
2:10	73	5:4-5.12	102
2:10-14	76	5:6	145
2:12-13	106	5:6-8	111
2:12-20	76	5:7	74
2:13	67	5:7b-8a	161, 171, 182
2:15	52	5:9	22
2:16	112	5:9.11	137
3:1	45, 112	5:9-11	39
3:1-3	148	5:9-13	101, 102
3:2	21, 127	5:10-11	124
3:2-4.22	45	5:12	113
3:3.6	76	5:13	102
3:4.6.22	30	6:1-11	101
3:5	135	6:5-12	41
3:5.10	135	6:6	113
3:5-11.16	93	6:9	113
3:6	21, 73	6:9.10	73
3:6-8	50	6:9-10	124
3:8	30, 76	6:9-11	101
3:9	29, 156	6:11	74, 76, 102, 115, 117, 127
3:10	73	6:12	52, 96, 101
3:11	74	6:12.13	42
3:16	76	6:12-13	52
3:16-17	50	6:12-20	101, 102
3:16-23	165	6:13	53, 124
3:19	165	6:13.15.17	102
3:20	72	6:13c-15a.17-20	171
3:21	145	6:13-20	95
3:21-23	28	6:14	73
4:1-5	166	6:15	41, 74
4:3.5	46	6:16-17	25
4:4	72	6:17	128
4:4-7	106	6:18a	101
4:6	30, 45	6:18b	101
4:7	68, 145	6:18-19	137
4:10	150	6:19	76, 93, 102
4:10-13	136	7	50
4:11-13	146	7-8	99
4:14.17	112	7:1	22, 39, 41, 42, 52, 103
4:15	18, 135	7:1.25	28
4:15-16	146	7:1-16	102
4:17	22, 31, 39, 92, 137	7:1-40	102
4:18-19	137	7:4	103
4:19	22	7:4.13-14	103

201

Index of Scripture References

1 Corinthians (continued)
7:7	98, 99, 100, 173
7:7-8.25-26.36-38.40	103
7:10	52, 65
7:14	113
7:15	73
7:17	92, 103
7:18-24	102
7:20	103
7:21-23	19
7:24	103, 172
7:25-40	102
7:26	103
7:29	70
7:29-31	172
7:32-34	103
7:32-35	172
7:40	77
8	118, 181
8-10	96
8:1	28
8:1.4.8	52, 104
8:1.5.8	42
8:1-11:1	104
8:3	72
8:4	52
8:4-5.7	111
8:6	72, 74, 75, 116
8:7.10.12	104
8:9	96, 104
8:12	181
9	52
9:1-2	137
9:1-3	97
9:1-10:22	104
9:3-6	138
9:3-19	3
9:9	111
9:14	52, 65
9:15	65, 136
9:16	145
9:16-19.22-23	173
9:17	65
9:19	97
9:20-21	104
9:20-22	143
9:20-23	105
9:21	113
9:23	105, 143
9:24-25	15, 111
9:24-27	50
10	118, 181
10-11	53
10:1-6.10-11	181
10:1-11	111
10:1-13	52
10:5	73
10:13	72
10:14-22	95, 121
10:16.21	121
10:16-17	121, 168
10:17	95, 112, 118
10:18-20	111
10:20	26
10:21	120
10:23	52, 104
10:23-11:1	104
10:25	104
10:25.27.28.29	104
10:29-30	51
10:31	127
10:31-11:1	174
11	18, 50, 88, 106, 118
11:1	74, 136, 146
11:2	42, 52, 66, 105
11:2.16.23	118
11:2-16	28
11:2-34	105
11:3	74, 105
11:3.5.6.10	105
11:4-5	27, 118
11:5	50, 65
11:14.15	105
11:16	92
11:16-27.34	105
11:17-18	45
11:17-18.20.33-34	113
11:17-18.22.33	118
11:17-22	105
11:17-34	120
11:18	28, 118
11:18-19	28
11:19	45
11:21	120
11:23-24	120
11:23.26	66
11:23-26	52, 65, 105, 121, 127, 161, 168, 171, 182, 188
11:24	120
11:24-25	121
11:26	25, 120, 121
11:27-29	123
11:27-34	105
11:28-29	106

202

Index of Scripture References

11:32 .... 72, 113	14:19. 106
11:34 22	14:20. . . . . 45, 94
12. . . . . 53, 76, 106, 137	14:22. 106
12:1 . . . . 28, 52, 98, 182	14:23. . . . . 92, 113, 118
12:2-31. 94	14:23-25 143
12:4 . . . . 76, 98	14:23.26.40. 118
12:4-5. 29	14:26. . . . . 99, 113, 118, 127
12:4-6. 98	14:27-36 28
12:4.9.28.30.31. 98	14:33. 73
12:4-11. 182	14:33-36 . . . . 50, 96
12:5 98	14:34-36 106
12:6 72	14:34-37 65
12:6a 98, 99	14:37. 52
12:6b 99	14:4-19. 27
12:6.13. 128	14:7-8.10-11 50
12:7 77	15 . . . . 53, 125
12:11 70	15:1-11 185
12:12 . . . . 28, 93	15:1-19. 66
12:12-13. . . . . 70, 117	15:1-58 75
12-14 . . . . 106, 143, 182	15:3. . . . . 74, 137
12:12-27. 106	15:3-4 . . . . 66, 69, 126
12:12-30. 183	15:3-7 52
12:13 . . . . 20, 25, 76, 87,	15:3-8 65
. . . . 95, 97, 98, 116, 117	15:3-8.11 185
12:13.27. 127	15:4.12 46
12:22-24. 95	15:4.12.20. 74
12:26 95	15:7-11 136
12:27 74	15:9. 3
12:28 . . . . 31, 73, 183	15:9-10. 137
12:28-31. 27	15:10. . . . . 73, 100
12:29-30. 100	15:11. 46
12:31 . . . . 52, 99, 107	15:12. . . . . 52, 126
12:31-13:13 184	15:12.16-20. 186
13. . . . . 96, 106	15:12-15 28
13:1 . . . . 13, 50	15:15. . . . . 73, 75
13:1-2.4-6. 106	15:18. 75
13:3 52	15:20-26a.28. 166
13:4-13. 184	15:20-28.45. 74
13:4-7. 96	15:21-22 69
13:9-12. 127	15:23-28 . . . . 51, 166
14. . . . . 76, 106, 118	15:24. 72
14:1.3.5.12 107	15:24.50 73
14:1-40. 118	15:27. 73
14:2-12. 113	15:28. 74
14:3 155	15:29. 116
14:3.19.31 113	15:30-32.58. 126
14:12 . . . . 93, 155	15:32. 126
14:12-15:26 128	15:37. . . . . 50, 73
14:13.27-28 106	15:40-41 50
14:13-15. 127	15:40-44 25
14:13-16. 114	15:45-49 187
14:18.22. 46	15:47. 74

203

1 Corinthians (continued)
15:51 . . . . 66, 67, 70, 172
15:52 . . . . 50, 126, 187
15:52-53 70
15:53 73
15:54-58 187
15:57 73
15:58 154
16:1 . . . . 92, 107, 112
16:1.5 134
16:1-4 107
16:2-4 107
16:2-7 22
16:3-5 39
16:5 . . . . 22, 137
16:8 22
16:10 22
16:10.17-18 39
16:10-11 31
16:12 30
16:13.22 127
16:14 96
16:15 . . . . 30, 85
16:15-16 . . . . 30, 138
16:17-19 134
16:19 . . . . 31, 85
16:20 112
18:24-19:1 30

2 Corinthians
1-9 . . . . 44, 48, 124
1:1 112
1:1.19 31
1:1-11 92
1:2 135
1:2-3 72
1:3 72
1:3-7 . . . . 113, 127
1:5-8 137
1:8 52
1:9 73
1:11 . . . . 98, 127, 128
1:12.14 145
1:13 39
1:16 22
1:18 72
1:18-22 174
1:19 . . . . 32, 74
1:21 115
1:21-22 112
1:24 137
2:1 22
2:1-2 39

2:3-4.9 22
2:4 . . . . 18, 22, 39
2:5-8 124
2:10 124
2:12-13 32
2:14 50
2:17 . . . . 50, 65, 135, 137
3:1 46
3:1b-6 175
3:4 74
3:5-6 143
3:6 77
3:12 143
3:14 113
3:16-18 116
3:17 . . . . 76, 96
3:18 76
4:1 72
4:1-3 143
4:2 142
4:3 113
4:3-4 67
4:4 . . . . 26, 71, 74
4:4-6 116
4:5 . . . . 65, 74, 141
4:6 . . . . 66, 73, 136
4:6-11 175
4:7 . . . . 3, 13, 50, 154
4:7-14 117
4:7-5:1 127
4:7-5:10 126
4:8-9 . . . . 25, 147
4:8-10 146
4:8-12 100
4:10-11 75
4:13 66
4:13-5:1 176
4:16 148
4:17-18 71
5:1 50
5:1.4 50
5:1-5 51
5:2.4 50
5:4.15.21 74
5:5 76
5:6-10 177
5:7 . . . . 68, 147
5:11 72
5:12 46
5:13 18
5:14 . . . . 75, 96
5:14-17 177

Index of Scripture References

Reference	Page(s)
5:16	68
5:17	28, 66, 70, 71, 76, 92, 112
5:17-19	43
5:17-21	181
5:18	72
5:18-19	73, 123
5:18-20	137
5:19	69
5:20	28, 123
5:21	66, 123, 124, 178
6:4-8	143
6:4-10	150
6:5	3
6:8-10	146, 147
6:9-10	51
6:14	113
6:16	72, 93
6:17	113
6:18	73
7:2	18
7:4	145
7:4-7	143
7:5-16	32
7:6.14-15	22
7:6-7	39
7:8.12	22, 39
7:15-16	32
8	107
8-9	107
8:1	73
8:2.3.13-14	107
8:4	112
8:6.16-19.23	178
8:7.9.13-15	178
8:9	74
8:14	137
8:16-19	22, 39
8:16-23	32
8:17	32
9	107
9:1-15	143
9:2-4	134, 178
9:7	73
9:8	73
9:9.11	107
9:11	108
9:15	73
10-11	28
10-13	22, 39, 44, 49, 51, 133, 141, 179
10:1	22, 143
10:4-13	50
10:8	155
10:8-13	145
10:9	22
10:10	3, 39, 152
10:12.18	46
10:13	50
10:13-14	137
10:14	22, 65
10:17	145
11-12	46
11:1-12:13	179
11:2	18
11:4	67, 145
11:5	46, 136, 141
11:5-11	143
11:6-7.11	134
11:13	46
11:14	179
11:22	26, 47
11:22-23	142
11:23-29	3
11:28	141
11:30	145
11:31	72-73
11:32	22
12:1-9	142
12:1-10	127
12:6	29
12:7-10	179
12:8-10	127
12:9	25, 74
12:9-10	138, 149
12:10	150
12:11	145
12:12	22, 143
12:14	22, 39
12:18	39
12:20-21	101
13:1.10	22
13:3-4	29
13:4	150
13:5	76, 152
13:6	18
13:7	127
13:9	25, 127
13:11	44, 112
13:11-13	167
13:12	112, 114
13:13	72, 73, 74, 76

Galatians

Reference	Page(s)
1:12-16	136
1:13.23	3

205

Index of Scripture References

Galatians (continued)
1:14 3
2:1-3 32
2:1-10 3
2:11-21 3
3:28 . . . . 20, 25, 87, 97, 116

Ephesians
5:21-6:9 91

Philippians
3:5 3
3:6 3
4:12 25

Colossians
3:10-11 97
3:10-12 116
3:18-4:1 91

4:15 85

1 Thessalonians
1:1 32
4:16 51
5:27 113

2 Thessalonians
1:1 32

1 Timothy
2:1-6:2 91

2 Timothy
4:19 85
4:20 32

Philemon
1-2 85

Index of Authors Cited

Banks, Robert 20, 29, 70, 92, 95, 97, 99, 100, 115, 119, 141
Barrett, C. K. 41, 42, 45, 46, 85, 103, 116, 138, 139
Beker, Christian J. 66, 68, 70, 75, 136, 146
Bornkamm, Gunther 4, 124
Branick, Vincent 86, 91, 92, 119
Brunt, John C. 104
Carlson, Richard P. 116, 117
Conzelmann, Hans 148
Corrigan, Gregory 151
Crosby, Michael H. 86
Doohan, Helen 28, 51, 76, 93, 127, 128, 153
Doohan, Leonard 66, 127, 128, 129, 153
Ellis, E. Earle 53, 122, 126
Fallon, Francis T. 43, 147
Filson, Floyd 83, 87
Fiorenza, Elisabeth Schussler 32, 52, 71, 85, 86, 87, 91, 92, 97, 116
Fisher, James A. 147
Fitzmeyer, Joseph A. 53
Furnish, Victor P. 41, 44, 46, 116, 123, 142
Gager, J. 96
Georgi, Dieter 47, 138
Gillman, Florence 32
Hahn, Ferdinand 98
Harrington, Daniel 155

Holmberg, Bengt 20, 31, 108
Hooker, Morna D. 105, 106
Horsley, Richard A. 104
Hurd, J. C. 42, 96, 103
Jeffers, James S. 91
Kee, Howard Clark 4
Kendall, Daniel 138
Kim, Seyoon 65, 74, 116, 135
Lampe, Peter 75, 149
LaVerdiere, Eugene 27
Love, Stuart 86, 88
Malina, Bruce 151
Martin, Ralph P. 77
Meeks, Wayne A. 18, 19, 25, 30, 42, 66, 74, 75, 77, 92, 102, 113, 115, 116, 119, 120, 125, 129
Meyers, Eric M. 86
Murphy-O'Connor, Jerome 13, 15, 16, 18, 19, 21, 22, 42, 46, 88, 93, 96, 101, 102, 103, 104, 107, 116, 121
Nardoni, Enrique 98
O'Day, Gail R. 149
O'Meara, Thomas Franklin 16
Papahatzis, Nicos 12, 14, 15
Patte, Daniel 67, 68
Peterson, Norman R. 79, 136
Plevnik, Joseph 68
Richardson, P. 105
Ridderbos, Herman 53, 71, 76, 93, 95, 98, 112, 114, 115, 125

Index of Authors Cited

Roetzel, Calvin J. 46, 108, 145
Sampley, J. Paul 94, 108
Schmithals, Walter 136
Stendahl, Krister 96
Swain, Lionel 75
Theissen, Gerd 19, 29, 46
Thrall, Margaret E. 148

Verner, David C. 91
Welborn, L. L. 16
Wire, Antionette Clark 52, 75, 96, 97, 103, 105, 106, 116, 117, 138, 148
Ziesler, John 74, 76

Index of Subjects

Acts of Apostles 2, 3, 8, 21, 29
  speeches in 66
apocalyptic 26, 70, 166, 187
Apollos 21, 27, 30, 31, 42, 45,
  155, 156
apostles 31, 135-146, 151, 155,
  184, 190
  authority of 136
  false 46-47
apostleship 28, 136, 145
Aquila 21, 31, 85, 137, 155, 156
assembly 28, 45, 50, 93, 105-106,
  118-120, 127, 168
authority 47, 91
baptism 19, 54, 95, 96, 97, 101,
  112, 114-117, 127, 181, 183
boasting 4, 28, 44, 46, 59, 134,
  138, 142, 143, 145, 179
body of Christ 99, 117, 118, 184
  as symbol 51
  community as the 28, 70, 74, 95,
    101, 106, 121, 122, 171
  unity of the 42, 45, 50, 94, 116,
    182, 183-184
call 30, 65, 103, 135-137,
  146-152, 163, 166, 172, 181
celibacy 28, 42, 84, 103, 172, 173
Cephas 185
charism(s) 98-100, 128
Christian life 6, 28, 48, 50, 51, 68,
  69, 71, 72, 75, 76, 77, 83, 94,
  102,˙117, 124-125, 127, 135,
  136, 142, 152, 168, 170, 172,
  174, 177, 185, 187, 190
  paradoxes of 51, 134, 146-151,
    163, 170-171, 176, 190
Christian love 19, 42, 71, 84, 94,
  96, 97, 99, 101, 106, 107, 108,
  122, 124, 134, 143, 144, 155,
  167, 178, 179, 182, 184-185
Christians as models 145, 174
church
  collaboration in 51, 155-156,
    182, 185
  mission of the 134
  model(s) of 51, 93
  partnership in 155-156, 183, 184
  unity of 45
collection for the poor 32, 43, 84,
  107-108, 178-179
conscience 104, 108, 181
Corinth, household(s) in 17, 20,
  31, 83, 92, 111, 115, 118-119,
  155, 161
Corinthian church
  diversity of 12, 18, 19, 26, 87, 95
  faith of 12, 24, 49, 50, 64, 84,
    126, 153, 178, 186, 188
  issues of 12, 16, 22, 28, 37, 41,
    48, 68, 69, 71, 84, 100, 162
  Paul's love for 39
  stratification of 18, 19-21, 26,
    45, 87

209

Index of Subjects

cross 26, 51, 58, 66, 73, 75, 139, 142, 146, 149, 151, 162, 163, 170
  power of 65, 149
discernment 28, 42, 84, 94, 97, 100, 102, 104, 106, 108, 109, 138, 144, 148, 152, 183
disciples 8, 29, 133-157, 162, 165, 190
diversity 27, 70, 72, 93, 120, 129, 143, 146, 155, 163, 183, 189
  of gifts 100, 144, 182-184
  value of 95
end times 26, 68, 70, 77
Ephesus 21, 22, 30, 41, 85
equality 9, 25, 29, 32, 58, 68, 70, 84, 91, 92, 94, 97, 101, 103, 105, 108, 117, 135, 178
ethical behavior 28
ethics 53, 104, 107, 108-109
Eucharist 46, 105, 112, 120-123, 161, 181
exhortations 37, 48, 64, 134, 143
faith 26, 76, 77, 104, 117, 125, 127, 137, 147, 150, 164, 170, 175, 176-177, 185, 189, 190
  as evoked by symbols 51
  building 93
  celebrations of 59
  challenges to 77
  gift of 65, 146, 166
  mystery of 75
  proclamation of 63
  spirit of 66
folly/foolishness 9, 134, 142, 148-149, 163, 165, 170
freedom 9, 25, 68, 70, 71, 76, 84, 94, 95, 96-97, 101, 102, 103, 105, 107, 108, 117, 123, 173
Gallio 21
Gentiles 2, 5, 25-26, 63, 66, 78, 94, 101, 107, 136, 156, 170
gifts 30-31, 73, 117, 118 *See also* Spirit, gifts of
Gospel
  Apollos' understanding of 31
  appeal of the 19
  Corinthian church's understanding of the 12, 58
  interpretation of the 14, 65, 98, 144, 164, 188
  living the 84, 94, 165, 177, 189

Paul's preaching of the 2, 3, 8, 18, 21, 24, 27, 37, 39, 41, 48, 59, 64-71, 87, 115, 134, 149, 152, 155, 159, 175, 190
Paul's understanding of the 77, 136
proclamation of 14, 29, 188
response to the 60
honor 134, 150-151, 152, 163, 184
  Paul's 145
honors, renouncement of 20
hope 9, 24, 26, 38, 43, 71, 125-127, 143, 154, 167, 170, 176-177, 187, 190
house churches 83-92, 103, 105, 106
  diversity in 87
  faith of 83, 87
idols 28, 42, 84, 96, 104, 168, 181
imitation 145
immorality 16, 28, 39, 42, 101
Isthmian games 14, 17, 50
Jerusalem 3, 32, 39, 47, 94, 107, 178
Jesus as model 44, 136, 175
Junia 32, 137
kerygma 52, 63, 66
kingdom of God 73, 136, 166-167
leadership 27, 31, 86, 92, 105, 119, 128, 137, 156, 174, 189
letters of Paul 29
  authenticity of 6-7, 37
  integrity of 7, 38
  theology in 48
liturgical ministry 46, 51, 68, 78
liturgy 20, 27, 29, 43, 49, 53, 54, 58, 59, 60, 65, 91, 111-129, 159, 188
Lord's Supper 18, 19, 42, 45, 53, 87, 95, 105, 120-123, 161, 168
marriage 28, 42, 49, 84, 103, 129, 138, 172
ministry 2, 4, 20, 28, 29, 32, 42, 43, 47, 77, 109, 117, 128, 133-157, 170, 175-176, 177, 182, 188, 190
  authentic 44, 141, 142
  gifts of 53
  mission 135-137, 151, 153-157
  of early church 32
  partnership in 135

210

Index of Subjects

missionaries 46, 63, 86, 103, 133, 135-146, 153, 155, 172, 175
Olympic games 14
paradox *See* Christian life, paradoxes of
parousia 166-167
Paul's portrayal of 50
patriarchy 49-50, 87, 91
Paul
  and coworkers 29-33, 41, 43, 63, 134, 135, 155
  apostleship of 44, 137-138, 162, 164, 166, 173, 185
  as a model 42, 68, 94, 150
  as apostle to the Gentiles 5, 49, 67, 143
  as missionary 3, 11, 17, 25, 26, 48, 68, 134, 154
  authority of 20, 24, 41, 47, 58
  call of 4-6
  conversion of 3, 4, 6, 20, 65, 67, 77
  faith of 6, 67, 69, 75, 78, 136
  imitation of 134, 145-146
  integrity of 59
  leadership of 28, 47, 78, 99, 189-190
  ministry of 8, 18, 22, 23, 28, 43, 46, 48, 59, 64, 65, 67, 71, 127, 139, 145, 146, 150, 164, 173, 174, 175, 179
  mission of 4-5, 29, 42, 65
  missionary journeys of 21, 32
  opposition to 18, 43, 45-47, 51, 58, 64, 68, 127, 134, 138, 145, 173, 175, 179
  Pharisaic background of 3, 5, 26, 67
  sufferings of 126, 136, 137, 142, 176
  theology of 5, 28, 37, 42, 51, 52, 53, 58, 64, 65, 66, 67-71, 74, 75, 77, 79, 149, 154
  vision of 97
Peter 3, 136
Phoebe 14, 32, 156
power 27, 28, 31, 47, 54, 75, 134, 139, 147, 149-150, 152, 162, 163, 164, 170
  of God 29, 53, 64, 73-74, 77, 92, 123, 142, 144, 150, 176, 177, 179
  of the Spirit 76
Prisca (Priscilla) 21, 31, 85, 137, 155, 156
prophecy 27, 29, 100, 105-106, 118, 128, 183, 185
prophet(s) 31, 32, 74, 136, 149, 152, 162, 184
  women 100, 105, 107, 138
reconciliation 28, 38, 71, 73, 112, 123-125, 181-182, 190
  between God and the world 69
  between Paul and the Corinthians 43, 48, 59
responsibility 53, 77, 83, 93, 94, 95, 96, 97, 98, 100, 102, 103, 104, 105, 108, 119, 124, 125, 128, 144, 155, 179, 184
resurrection 26, 28, 42, 46, 53, 71, 75-76, 78, 102, 126, 146, 166, 171, 176, 185-186, 187-188
  Paul's belief in the 26
  Paul's portrayal of the 50, 51, 69
  power of the 74
  transformational significance of the 49, 75
ritual 19, 25, 27, 63, 86, 87, 92, 113, 115, 116-117, 121-122, 125, 127, 129, 168
Rome 21, 31, 85
salvation 68, 69, 70, 71, 74, 162, 181, 182
second coming 51, 66, 172
service 30, 128, 134, 136, 138, 143, 144, 154, 161, 175, 183
shame 150-151, 163
social status 103
Spirit
  as life-giving 77
  gifts of the 26, 27, 42, 45, 46, 70, 76-77, 83, 84, 95, 98-100, 105, 106-107, 116, 118, 119, 120, 128, 143, 151, 154, 156, 170, 178, 182-183, 184
  transformative power of the 76
spirituality 144
suffering 54, 71, 95, 97, 142, 146
symbols 51
theology 27, 47, 138
Thessalonians (1 and 2) 31

Index of Subjects

tradition 25, 26, 52, 66, 77, 78, 114, 126, 135, 137, 156, 181, 185, 188
  apostolic 65
transformation 4, 5, 28, 49, 53, 54, 70-71, 94, 99, 114-117, 123, 124, 126, 127, 135, 150, 151, 166, 176, 177, 182, 185, 187, 190
unity 53, 70, 71, 84, 93, 94-95, 96, 97, 99, 101, 105, 106, 107, 108, 122, 134, 143, 155, 161, 163, 167, 178
values 8, 21, 91, 94, 96, 100, 134, 145, 151, 165, 167, 170-171, 178
vision of early church 153, 156

weakness 53, 75, 134, 139, 149-150, 163, 176, 179
wisdom 9, 16, 26, 27, 42, 45, 46, 58, 74, 134-135, 138, 147, 148-149, 152, 162, 163, 164-165, 170, 183
  of God 73-74, 142, 143
women 14, 20, 42, 58, 59, 84, 91, 96, 97, 103, 106, 155
  leadership of in early church 32, 85, 105, 119
  role of in church 28, 50, 59, 87
worship 7, 42, 59, 84, 87, 93, 95, 113, 119, 120, 122, 127-129, 190
  and life, connection between 42, 111-112, 114, 168

www.ingramcontent.com/pod-product-compliance
Lightning Source LLC
Chambersburg PA
CBHW060604230426
43670CB00011B/1966